MW00637794

American
English in Mind

Herbert Puchta & Jeff Stranks
with Peter Lewis-Jones

Workbook **4**

CAMBRIDGE
UNIVERSITY PRESS

CAMBRIDGE UNIVERSITY PRESS
Cambridge, New York, Melbourne, Madrid, Cape Town,
Singapore, São Paulo, Delhi, Mexico City

Cambridge University Press
32 Avenue of the Americas, New York, NY 10013-2473, USA

www.cambridge.org
Information on this title: www.cambridge.org/9780521733489

First published 2011
2nd printing 2013

Printed in Hong Kong, China, by Sheck Wah Tong Printing Press Limited

A catalog record for this publication is available from the British Library.

ISBN 978-0-521-73347-2 Student's Book 4
ISBN 978-0-521-73348-9 Workbook 4
ISBN 978-0-521-73349-6 Teacher's Edition 4
ISBN 978-0-521-73357-1 Class Audio 4
ISBN 978-0-521-73337-3 Classware 4
ISBN 978-0-521-73358-8 Testmaker 4
ISBN 978-0-521-73370-0 DVD 4

Art direction, book design and layout: Pentacor plc
Photo research: Copyright Works Inc.

Contents

1 Challenging lives

1 Grammar review

★ Past tense review

a Underline the correct option.

I [1]*watched / was watching* Rain Man at home the other day when part of a conversation in the movie really [2]*caught / was catching* my attention. In fact, I [3]*was / had been* so surprised that I watched the scene again to make sure I [4]*was hearing / had heard* it correctly. In the movie, the character Raymond Babbitt, who is autistic, claimed that Qantas was the only airline that [5]*never had / had never had* a crash. I [6]*went / had gone* online to check out this fact. Apparently, it wasn't 100 percent true. When the movie was made, Qantas [7]*had had / was having* eight crashes, but they [8]*were all being / had all been* propeller planes, not jets. I also [9]*found / had found* out that all airlines (except Qantas, of course) [10]*took / were taking* this line out of the movie when they [11]*were showing / showed* it on flights at the time.

★ be used to + gerund vs. used to + base form

b Rewrite the sentences using the correct form of *used to*.

1 My dad was a doctor, but he retired five years ago.
   My dad used to be a doctor, but he retired five years ago.

2 I don't usually get up so early.
   ....

3 When I was a teenager, I rode my bike everywhere.
   ....

4 When I first arrived in South Korea, I thought it was strange to bow to people when I met them.
   ....

5 My grandmother always told us great bedtime stories when we were young.
   ....

6 He's a pilot, so he doesn't find it difficult to work long hours.
   ....

7 He was my friend, but we had an argument.
   ....

8 Since I've been in Italy, I've been drinking strong coffee.
   ....

★ should / should have

c Complete the sentence with *should(n't)* or *should(n't) have* and the verb in parentheses.

1 If you're not feeling well, you __should lie__ down for a while. (lie)

2 You .... him yourself. Then he wouldn't have been so upset when he found out from Sandra. (tell)

3 It's really hot out there today. You .... a hat with you if you don't want to get sunburned. (take)

4 I'm not surprised he had an accident. He .... when there was so much snow. (drive)

5 I think we .... food with us on our hike. I'm starting to get really hungry. (bring)

6 You .... this movie by yourself. It's really scary! (watch)

✱ *wish*

d Write sentence about what these people might be wishing.

1 I ate so much, and now I feel sick.

   I wish I hadn't eaten so much.

2 I just haven't had enough time to do everything.

   ----

3 Why can't it be Saturday?

   ----

4 I really wanted to see that movie, but it's not playing at the movie theater anymore.

   ----

5 I worry about everything. It's really annoying.

   ----

6 I gave that dog my hamburger, and now it's following me home.

   ----

7 Why didn't I tell the truth? Now, I'm in big trouble.

   ----

8 I wonder what she's thinking. I'd love to know.

   ----

② Pronunciation

✱ Thought groups

a ▶ **CD4 T02** Listen and mark the pauses /ˆ/ in the sentences.

1 The important thing ˆ is to understand your weaknesses.

2 You need to realize that sometimes you need to work harder at some things than others.

3 In many ways, you can learn a lot from your mistakes.

4 Making a mistake can sometimes be the best thing you can do.

5 Once you have more life experience, you will learn how to deal with your shortcomings.

b ▶ **CD4 T02** Listen again and repeat.

③ Vocabulary

✱ Personality adjectives

a Match the words with their definitions.

1	bossy	_d_	a	doesn't think about other people's feelings and emotions
2	considerate	....	b	has a lot of good ideas and is very creative
3	insensitive	....	c	always does the practical thing, never does anything silly
4	bad-tempered	....	d	tells others what to do all the time
5	imaginative	....	e	likes to do things on his own, doesn't need help from others
6	sensible	....	f	follows a plan even if it is difficult
7	independent	....	g	wants a lot from life
8	ambitious	....	h	thinks about others and how they might be feeling
9	determined	....	i	easily upset by things others think and say
10	sensitive	....	j	never in a good mood, always angry about something

✱ *make* and *do*

b Complete the sentences with the correct form of *make* or *do*.

My brother Kyle really hasn't ____*made*____ any progress this year at school. He [1] _____ very badly on his tests all year. And his homework didn't [2] _____ any sense at all.

I think Kyle's real problem is that he never tries to [3] _____ his best. If he [4] _____ more of an effort to listen to the teacher and spent less time [5] _____ fun of other people, it might [6] _____ all the difference.

c Complete the text with the missing prepositions.

Whenever a big problem comes ___up___ , it's always a good idea to think it [1] _____ for a while and try to sort it [2] _____ on your own. If you still can't make [3] _____ your mind about what to do, then you might want to talk it [4] _____ with a friend. If that doesn't make the problem go [5] _____ then maybe you should try and sleep [6] _____ it and come [7] _____ to it in the morning. You might find a solution that you didn't think of the day before.

✱ Friends

d Match the sentence halves.

Friends forever — a declaration of friendship

1 I will always stand ___e___   a on you. Your secrets are safe with me.

2 I will never tell ....   b out or argue about anything.

3 I will always stick ....   c up for you when others are being mean.

4 I will never let ....   d along well forever.

5 We will never fall ....   e by you no matter what you do.

6 We will get ....   f you down. I'll always be by your side.

✱ Phrasal verbs and friends

e Underline the phrasal verbs in the poem. There is one in each line.

Friends Forever?

[1] When we have a problem, you
     say, "Go away."

[2] "Let's talk over the problem,"
     is what I always say.

[3] If I do something wrong, you
     usually tell on me.

[4] I always stand by you, which
     is better, don't you agree?

[5] If a problem comes up, you
     sometimes scream and shout.

[6] I like to discuss our problems
     and try to sort them out.

[7] Somehow we always make up,
     and we stay friends.

[8] Despite our differences, we get
     along in the end.

4 Fiction in mind

a Read more of *The Curious Incident of the Dog in the Night-Time*. Christopher was taken to the police station after he found the dead dog and hit the policeman. Do the police punish him?

At 1:28 a.m. a policeman opened the door of the cell and told me that there was someone to see me.

I stepped outside. Father was standing in the corridor. He held up his right hand and spread his fingers out in a fan. I held up my left hand and spread my fingers out in a fan and we made our fingers and thumbs touch each other. We do this because sometimes Father wants to give me a hug, but I do not like hugging people so we do this instead, and it means that he loves me.

Then the policeman told us to follow him down the corridor to another room. In the room was a table and three chairs. He told us to sit down on the far side of the table and he sat down on the other side. There was a tape recorder on the table and I asked whether I was going to be interviewed and he was going to record the interview.

He said, "I don't think there will be any need for that."

He was an inspector. I could tell because he wasn't wearing a uniform. He also had a very hairy nose. It looked as if there were two very small mice hiding in his nostrils.

He said, "I have spoken to your father and he says that you didn't mean to hit the policeman."

I didn't say anything because this wasn't a question.

He said, "Did you mean to hit the policeman?"

I said, "Yes."

He squeezed his face and said, "But you didn't mean to hurt the policeman?"

I thought about this and said, "No. I didn't mean to hurt the policeman. I just wanted him to stop touching me."

Then he said, "You know that it is wrong to hit a policeman, don't you?"

I said, "I do."

He was quiet for a few seconds, then he asked, "Did you kill the dog, Christopher?"

I said, "I didn't kill the dog."

He said, "Do you know that it is wrong to lie to a policeman and that you can get into a very great deal of trouble if you do?"

I said, "Yes."

He said, "So, do you know who killed the dog?"

I said, "No."

He said, "Are you telling the truth?"

I said, "Yes. I always tell the truth."

And he said, "Right. I am going to give you a caution."

I asked, "Is that going to be on a piece of paper like a certificate I can keep?"

He replied, "No, a caution means that we are going to keep a record of what you did, that you hit a policeman but that it was an accident and that you didn't mean to hurt the policeman."

I said, "But it wasn't an accident."

And my father said, "Christopher, please."

The policeman closed his mouth and breathed out loudly through his nose and said, "If you get into any more trouble we will take out this record and see that you have been given a caution and we will take things much more seriously. Do you understand what I am saying?"

I said that I understood.

b Read the text again. Mark the sentences *T* (true) or *F* (false).

1 Christopher's father hugs him when he sees him. ..... *F*

2 Christopher's father goes into the room with Christopher and the investigator. ....

3 The investigator records the interview on a tape recorder. ....

4 Christopher says hitting the policeman wasn't an accident. ....

5 Christopher gets a certificate after the interview. ....

6 The investigator writes down what Christopher did. ....

5 Write

a Read part of the conversation Christopher and his father had on the way home from the police station in *The Curious Incident of the Dog in the Night-Time*. Do you think Christopher will follow his father's advice?

There were clouds in the sky on the way home, so I couldn't see the Milky Way.

I said, "I'm sorry," because Father had to come to the police station, which was a bad thing.

He said, "It's OK."

I said, "I didn't kill the dog."

And he said, "I know."

Then he said, "Christopher, you have to stay out of trouble, OK?"

I said, "I didn't know I was going to get into trouble. I like Wellington and I went to say hello to him, but I didn't know that someone had killed him."

Father said, "Just try and keep your nose out of other people's business."

I thought for a little and I said, "I am going to find out who killed Wellington."

And Father said, …

b Read the conversation again. Who said these things? Mark the sentence *F* (Father) or *C* (Christopher).

1 "It's OK."   *F*

2 "I didn't kill the dog."   ....

3 "Just try and keep your nose out of other
    people's business."   ....

4 "I'm sorry."   ....

5 "I am going to find out who killed
    Wellington."   ....

6 "I know."   ....

c Now continue the story. Write 100–120 words and at least four more lines for Father and four more for Christopher. Add information about what they are doing or thinking in addition to the conversation.

WRITING TIP

Writing a conversation

- When you write a conversation, each person's words begin a new paragraph.

- When you write what someone said, be sure it is clear what people *he* and *she* refer to when using *he said* and *she said*.

- Both the past tense and the present tense are common in writing conversations. *She says, / She said,*

- Be sure to use the correct punctuation. Use a comma after a reporting verb, like *say* or *ask*. Use double quotation marks around what is said. The final period goes inside the quotation marks. *He said, "It's OK."*

Unit check

1 Fill in the spaces

Complete the text with the words in the box.

> determined   didn't speak   has written   imaginative   realized
> came back   stood by   used to be   ~~used to being~~   went away

As an award-winning writer, Maya Angelou is _used to being_ famous, but she had many challenges growing up. She went through a period of several years when she ¹ _____ , but once she started talking, she had a lot to say. She quit school when she was 14 to get a job. She was ² _____ , and she later went back to finish high school. Her brother always ³ _____ her. She graduated from high school and started working again. She ⁴ _____ a waitress and cook. However, she was always interested in art, music and writing. In 1954, she ⁵ _____ to be in a play in Europe. She then went on to study modern dance. In the early 1960s, she lived in Egypt and Ghana, but she eventually ⁶ _____ to the United States. In 1970, her book, *I Know Why the Caged Bird Sings,* was published. Maya Angelou is an ⁷ _____ writer. As soon as people ⁸ _____ this, her book became very popular. Since that time, she ⁹ _____ many books and has been in movies and on television.

| 9 |

2 Choose the correct answers

Circle the correct answer: a, b or c.

1 Jennifer _____ when Mia got home.
   a wrote   b (was writing)   c had written

2 Tom _____ and published a book last year.
   a wrote   b was writing   c had written

3 Oliver _____ since 1998.
   a didn't write   b wasn't writing   c hasn't written

4 My sister _____ a hard time in school, but now she's doing well.
   a used to have   b used to having   c use to have

5 Martin _____ such a bossy manager.
   a isn't use to have   b isn't used to having
   c isn't used to be

6 I _____ you would wait for me. I'm almost done.
   a wish   b wished   c was wishing

7 I wish you _____ told me that. I don't like to know secrets.
   a weren't having   b haven't   c hadn't

8 You _____ be more ambitious. Maybe you could take a class.
   a shouldn't have   b should   c should have

9 I _____ so insensitive. I didn't mean to hurt your feelings.
   a shouldn't have been   b shouldn't have   c shouldn't be

| 8 |

3 Vocabulary

Underline the correct words.

1 Why don't you sleep *on* / *up* / *for* it and decide tomorrow?

2 My sister and I usually get *back* / *out* / *along* well.

3 Let's sort *out* / *over* / *away* this problem before we leave.

4 If you have to talk to the boss, I'll stick *on* / *up* / *by* for you.

5 You really should think *about* / *away* / *out* it before you accept the job.

6 We'll come *for* / *along* / *back* to this issue in the morning.

7 Please don't tell *up* / *on* / *over* me. I didn't mean to do it.

8 We fight a lot, but we always make *up* / *along* / *on*.

9 Are you going *away* / *by* / *up* for work next week?

| 8 |

How did you do?

Total: | 25 |

| 🙂 | Very good 25 – 20 | 😐 | OK 19 – 16 | 🙁 | Review Unit 1 again 15 or less |

2 Getting into trouble

1 Grammar review

✱ Present perfect and future passive

a Make the sentences passive.

1 They've announced an exciting new reality show.

   An exciting new reality show has been announced.

2 They'll call the show *Focus Rally: America.*

   _____

3 They'll choose 12 people to drive across the United States in new Ford Focus cars.

   _____

4 They'll divide the contestants into teams of two people each.

   _____

5 They'll make the teams complete challenges on the trip.

   _____

6 They'll give $100,000 to the team that gets into the least trouble and wins.

   _____

7 They've auditioned people for the show in cities around the U.S.

   _____

8 They haven't picked the teams yet.

   _____

9 They won't show the episodes on TV, but on the Internet.

   _____

✱ Future predictions

b Complete the sentences so they are true about you.

In the next 10 years...

1 I'm not likely _____ .

2 I won't _____ .

3 I'll probably _____ .

4 I might _____ .

5 I probably won't _____ .

6 I'll _____ .

✱ make / let / be allowed to

c Complete the sentences with *(not) let, make* or *(not) be allowed to.*

1 They only _____*let*_____ me in the house at night. I stay in my doghouse outside during the day.

2 I _____ sleep on their bed even though it's the most comfortable place in the house.

3 They _____ me go for a walk every day – even when it's raining.

4 They _____ chase the cat, and they get really mad if I do.

5 They _____ me eat dog food, but I like people food better.

6 Sometimes I _____ eat their food, but not very often.

7 They _____ me watch TV, and my favorite show is *The Dog Whisperer.*

8 They know I don't like water, but they still _____ me take a bath once a week.

✱ Modals of deduction (past)

d Rewrite the <u>underlined</u> sentences using *might have, must have* or *couldn't have.*

1 Tim didn't know your secret. <u>I'm sure he didn't tell Olivia.</u>

 He couldn't have told Olivia.

2 It's a real antique. <u>I bet it cost a lot of money.</u>

 ....

3 <u>I'm not sure if I paid or not.</u> I can't remember.

 ....

4 She's a terrible singer. <u>I don't believe she got a record deal.</u>

 ....

5 She really loved that hat. <u>I'm sure she was upset when she lost it.</u>

 ....

6 Jake doesn't speak a word of Spanish. <u>There's no way he lived in Peru for six years.</u>

 ....

7 She's not talking to me. <u>Maybe I said something to upset her.</u>

 ....

8 You live next door to the crime scene. <u>I'm sure you heard something.</u>

 ....

2 Pronunciation

✱ Linking with silent /h/

a ▶ **CD4 T03** Listen and complete the sentences with the correct words.

1 I asked ......*her*...... if she saw the crime.
2 She didn't see it, but .... brother did.
3 I called .... to get the details.
4 The phone rang a lot, but .... never answered.
5 I left a message on .... voicemail.
6 I also sent .... a text, but .... never got back to me.

b ▶ **CD4 T03** Listen again and repeat.

3 Vocabulary

✱ Crimes

a What crimes were committed? Choose the words in the box.

arson ~~burglary~~ joyriding pick-pocketing shoplifting vandalism

1 While we were out, someone broke into our home and stole my mom's jewelry. ......*burglary*......
2 My friend took some CDs from a store without paying for them. ....
3 While I was on the bus, someone took money out of my pocket. ....
4 Some kids broke the windows at the school and then ran away. ....
5 A teenager took my car and drove it around without my permission. ....
6 That man set two houses on fire on purpose. ....

✱ Getting into trouble

b Complete the sentences with the words in the box.

> breaking   caught   committing   do   doing   ~~gotten~~   put   pay   sent

OK. So you've done it a few times and always have _____*gotten*_____ away with it. You know you're
¹ _____ something wrong, but you're not really ² _____ a crime, are you? Wrong!
Shoplifting is a crime that the police take seriously. And one day you will get ³ _____ .
Then what?

Well, that depends. You may have to ⁴ _____ a fine or ⁵ _____ community service.
Get caught a second time, and you'll be ⁶ _____ on probation. If you continue to shoplift, you
could be ⁷ _____ to prison. Shoplifting is serious. ⁸ _____ the law is not a joke!

✱ Television

c Match the words and the definitions.

1   series _____*e*_____   a   the person who introduces a TV show
2   contestant _____   b   statistics that show how many people watch a show
3   celebrity _____   c   the people who watch a TV show in the studio
4   host _____   d   the people who watch TV at home
5   ratings _____   e   a TV show that tells a story over several weeks/months
6   an episode _____   f   a famous person
7   audience _____   g   one part of a TV series
8   viewers _____   h   someone who competes in a TV game show

✱ Anger

d Complete the sentences with the words in the box.

> ~~angry~~   bit   calm   cool   furious   headed   tantrum   temper

A bad day

The day got off to a bad start, and then it just got worse. My sister was _____*angry*_____ with me because
I spent too long in the bathroom. Then my dad ¹ _____ my head off just because I started reading
the paper before him. Honestly, he's so hot-² _____ . At least my other sister didn't shout at me.
But then she hasn't said anything to me for about a week now. She's mad at me, too, but she's stayed very
³ _____ . I almost wish she would tell me why she's mad! As I was leaving the house, my baby
brother started having a ⁴ _____ . I left that for my mom to deal with.

School wasn't much better. My best friend Lucy lost her ⁵ _____ with me just because I told Brian
that she was having party. I didn't know that she didn't invite him. I told her to keep her ⁶ _____ ,
but that just made things worse. Finally, Mr. Peterson got absolutely ⁷ _____ with me because I
was talking during his class. I was only telling Brian that Lucy was having a party. Hopefully, tomorrow will
be better!

e Read the text in Exercise 3d again. Then number the pictures in the correct order.

Read

a Read the text. Complete the sentences with one word in each space. There is often more than one possibility.

In the 1970s, Arnold Shapiro ___*made*___ a movie called *Scared Straight*. Seventeen teenagers were ¹_____ in a prison for a day in New Jersey in the United States. They spent the day with real prisoners who committed serious ²_____ . The program was to deter the teenagers from a life of crime in the ³_____ . The movie was popular and led to four other movies that followed the 17 teenagers. The movies showed how the prison experience affected the teens. Fourteen of the teenagers said the experience ⁴_____ their lives, and they said they were ⁵_____ to stay out of prison. The movie also led to similar "scared straight" programs around the country.

In 2011, Shapiro started a TV series based on the same idea. The show is called *Beyond Scared Straight*. Each ⁶_____ features different young people in a different prison for a day. The participants in the

program are between 11 and 18 years old. Youth counselors choose the participants. Some have committed minor crimes, like shoplifting. Others have already committed more ⁷_____ crimes, like ⁸_____ or arson. Some have only had warnings, and some have been arrested before. Shapiro hopes the experience will show young people what ⁹_____ is like and that they will choose not to commit crimes in the future. He also hopes teens watching the show will have a similar reaction.

The show is controversial. Many people think that young people can be "scared straight," and they will choose not to commit crimes after spending a day in prison. Some research shows that this method does not work. Some people think that these types of programs do more harm than ¹⁰_____ .

b ▶ **CD4 T04** Listen to the radio program. Five people give their opinions about the TV show *Beyond Scared Straight*. Check (✓) the correct column in the chart.

		Thinks the show is a good idea	Thinks the show is a bad idea
1	Tom	✓	
2	Victoria		
3	Laura		
4	Danny		
5	Carlos		

Skills in mind

5 Listen

a ▶ **CD4 T05** Listen and complete the tips.

Crime Prevention

Pick-pocketing

- Do not put valuable items in coat ___pockets___ or in the outside pockets of bags.
- Hold your [1] _____ close to you.
- Do not let anyone distract you.
- Avoid showing how much [2] _____ you have.

Burglary

- Lock your [3] _____ when you leave your home.
- Keep lights on in and outside your home when you are gone.
- Buy an [4] _____ system for your home.

Joyriding

- Park your car in a lighted area.
- [5] _____ lock your doors.
- Use an extra lock on the steering wheel of your car.

Personal attacks

- Don't walk [6] _____ , especially at night.
- Walk [7] _____ and confidently.
- Pay attention to your surroundings.
- Do not wear [8] _____ that others can see.

b ▶ **CD4 T05** Listen again. Write the category of crime for each prevention tip.

1 Make it a habit so you don't forget. _____Burglary_____

2 Travel in groups. _____

3 One person distracts you, and the other takes your items. _____

4 Don't talk on your phone while walking. _____

5 They follow people out of stores. _____

6 People who take them don't want to be seen. _____

Unit check

1 Fill in the spaces

Complete the text with the words in the box.

| furious   gangs   joyriding   let   made   ~~not allowed to~~   not likely   probably   trouble   refused |

My parents are really strict. For example, I'm __not allowed to__ stay out late at night. I also have to be home for dinner every night, although sometimes they ¹_____ me eat at a friend's house. I don't like it, but I understand why they're strict. There are a lot of problems with ²_____ in my neighborhood, and they just want me to be safe. One time, I ³_____ to follow the rules, and I stayed out with some new friends. We went ⁴_____ in a stolen car. I felt terrible when I finally got home. My parents were ⁵_____ with me, but they were glad I told them about it. I'm ⁶_____ to do that again. In fact, I ⁷_____ won't go out with those friends again. My parents ⁸_____ me apologize to the person who owned the car and help that person around her house for a month. I haven't gotten into ⁹_____ since.

| 9 |

2 Choose the correct answers

(Circle) the correct answer: a, b or c.

1 A new program ____ in our town to prevent crime.
  a (has been started) b been started
  c has been start

2 The new movie ____ on Friday night.
  a shows b will be shown c will show

3 I ____ report the crime to the police.
  a will probably b won't probably c likely to

4 Tanya ____ to get into trouble. She's never gotten into serious trouble before.
  a might get b will probably c isn't likely

5 Do your parents ____ you stay out late? I have to be home by 10:00.
  a are allowed to b make c let

6 We ____ have phones at school. It's against the rules.
  a make us b aren't allowed to c let us

7 Steve ____ stolen that car. He doesn't know how to drive.
  a couldn't have b must have c might have

8 My cousin ____ in prison. He committed arson, but I don't know what his punishment was.
  a was b couldn't have been
  c might have been

9 Julia ____ her lesson. She hasn't been shoplifting since she was caught.
  a didn't learn b couldn't have learned
  c must have learned

| 8 |

3 Vocabulary

Put the words and phrases in the correct place in the chart.

| audience   ~~arson~~   episode
hot-headed   ratings   shoplifting
tantrum   temper   vandalism |

Crimes	TV	Anger
arson		

How did you do?

| 8 |

Total: | 25 |

| 😃 | Very good 25 – 20 | 😐 | OK 19 – 16 | 🙁 | Review Unit 2 again 15 or less |

1 Grammar

✱ Relative clauses: review

a Complete the text about the singer Madonna with the correct relative pronouns.

Madonna is a singer, composer and actor _____*who*_____ was born in Bay City, Michigan in 1958. In 1977, she moved to New York [1] _____ she hoped to start her singing career. After a few months in New York she met a DJ, [2] _____ contacts at a record company gave Madonna the opportunity she was hoping for. "Holiday," [3] _____ was one of her first songs, became an international hit. She starred as Eva Perón in the film *Evita*, a role [4] _____ won her many awards. She is not afraid to sing songs [5] _____ are controversial. Madonna, [6] _____ personal life is always in the news, has four children. In 2001, she moved with her family to England, but in 2008, she moved back to the United States, [7] _____ she now lives. In 2005, her album *Confessions on a Dance Floor* went straight to number one in forty different countries, breaking a record [8] _____ , until then, had been held by the Beatles.

b Cross out the relative pronoun where it is unnecessary.

1 The concert ~~that~~ I wanted to go to had already sold out.

2 Those students who have passed their exams don't need to come to the review class.

3 The man who Tony was speaking to is my boss.

4 Saturday, which is my birthday, is also my day off.

5 The pasta that I had for lunch was delicious.

6 The sauce that came with the pasta was amazing.

7 I got an email from the lady who I contacted about the youth hostel.

8 I have to take a train that stops in Orlando.

9 The restaurant where we ate was very expensive.

10 The book that I'm reading is about the human mind.

c Circle the correct relative pronouns.

1 It's the first time (that) / what we've met, isn't it?

2 The girl who / whose place you're sitting in is coming back in a minute.

3 The place that / where I live is too quiet for me.

4 Everyone which / who replies will get a free CD.

5 What's the name of the movie that / who won the Oscar?

6 I took a computer class what / which was really helpful.

7 The girl which / whose dog ran away is in my class.

8 Did you understand that / what he was saying?

d Check (✓) the sentence, a or b, that goes with the first statement in **bold**.

1 **Not all the children got the flu.**
   a The children who went to the party got the flu. ☐
   b The children, who went to the party, got the flu. ☐

2 **They were looking for a sushi restaurant.**
   a They went into a restaurant which served sushi. ☐
   b They went into a restaurant, which served sushi. ☐

3 **I wanted to go to Florence.**
   a I booked the first vacation I found which was to Florence. ☐
   b I booked the first vacation I found, which was to Florence. ☐

4 **No one was allowed into the room.**
   a The people who were late weren't allowed into the room. ☐
   b The people, who were late, weren't allowed into the room. ☐

e Join the two sentences to make one sentence using relative pronouns.

1 He's taking a class. The class lasts for three months.

   He's taking a class that lasts for three months.

2 Kate won the tennis match. She played against Alicia.

   ....

3 I spoke to the man. The man works at the information desk.

   ....

4 Yesterday I met Jenny. Jenny's sister was in my class in college.

   ....

5 They've started training for the game. The game will decide the championship.

   ....

6 Shawn has moved to Chicago. He has lived next door to me for three years.

   ....

7 I asked him to mail the letter. I had written the letter to my cousin.

   ....

8 My brother booked a vacation to New York. He lived in New York for six months.

   ....

f Read the sentences. Some are correct and some have a word which should not be there. If a sentence is correct, put a check (✓) in the space at the end of the line. If a word should not be there, cross it out and write the word in the blank.

1 The girl who opened the door was her sister.   ....✓............

2 The person whose his car is blocking yours is over there.   ....

3 The place where I used to live that was called Oakview.   ....

4 There were some good bands at the concert that what I went to. ....

5 The bus that goes into town leaves from the corner.   ....

6 The company that it makes these products is based in China. ....

7 My sister used to go out with a guy who drove a Ferrari.

8 The guesthouse where we stayed it had a lovely view.   ....

2 Grammar

✻ Relative clauses with *which*

Match the two parts of the sentences. Write a–d in the boxes

1 You don't know what you're going to
  be asked on the day of the exam, ☐

2 Some scientists say men and women
  are becoming more alike, ☐

3 He moved to Vancouver last year, ☐

4 I need to buy a new car, ☐

a which means I'll have to start saving.

b which means that opportunities could
  become more equal.

c which means we hardly get to see him.

d which makes preparing for it very difficult.

3 Vocabulary

✱ Sports

a Complete the crossword using the clues 1–9.

Across

4 Where you play tennis.

6 What you do to the ball with your foot in soccer.

8 Glasses you wear when you are swimming.

9 You need one of these to hit the ball in tennis.

Down

1 What you hit with a stick in ice hockey.

2 For this sport, your board is no good if there aren't any waves.

3 The name of the grassy area you play soccer on.

5 You wear these when it's cold or if you're a boxer.

7 This protects your head in aggressive or dangerous sports.

9 Where you go to ice skate or to play ice hockey.

b (Circle) the correct words to complete the dialogue.

Raul: Who ¹*beat* / (*won*) the game on Saturday?

Julio: The Diamonds. They ²*beat* / *scored* the Reds with two goals to one.

Raul: Who ³*tied* / *scored*?

Julio: Jack Gordon ⁴*scored* / *won* the first goal. The Reds got a goal back, and it looked like they were going to ⁵*tie* / *win* in the end.

Raul: Then what happened?

Julio: Five minutes before the end, one of the Reds' defenders was ⁶*beaten* / *ejected* and the Diamonds got a penalty kick, which Gordon ⁷*beat* / *scored*. But if that player hadn't been ejected, I don't think the Reds would have ⁸*beat* / *lost*.

4 Pronunciation

✱ Intonation in questions

a Look at the questions. Do you think the voice goes up ↑ or down ↓ at the end of each one of them?

1 What time does the flight take off?
   In about half an hour.

2 Are you going away for the weekend?
   No, I'm staying at home.

3 Do you want to go for a drive in my new car?
   I'd love to.

4 Where do we get off the bus for the museum?
   It's the next stop.

5 Will you send me a postcard when you get there?
   Of course I will.

6 Are you leaving for Paris tonight?
   Yes, at about ten thirty.

b ▶ CD4 T06 Listen and check.

c ▶ CD4 T06 Listen again and repeat the questions.

5 Culture in mind

a This is part of a web page about a sport called lacrosse. Read the text and match.

1 crosse
2 attackmen
3 face-off
4 body checking

a the players who usually score the goals
b when two players start the game to see who gets the ball first
c bumping other players between the waist and the shoulders
d the short name for the stick used in the game

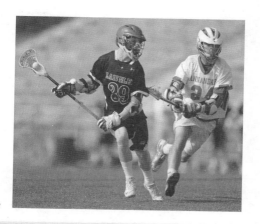

⯇ ⯈ C ⌂ http://www.sportsinfo.cup/lacrosse

SportsInfo   definitions   top searches   news   discussions

Lacrosse

Lacrosse is an outdoor team sport of Native American origin. It is primarily played on the East Coast of the United States and in Canada. It is played with rackets called lacrosse sticks, *crosses* for short, and a rubber ball. The crosses are long sticks with triangular nets on one end used to catch, carry and throw the ball. The crosses are different lengths depending on the position of the team member. There are short crosses that are about a meter long, and there are long crosses that are 1.3 to 1.8 meters long. Lacrosse is played on a field that is 100 meters long and 55 meters wide. In addition, there are goals at either end that are 1.8 meters by 1.8 meters with nets. All players wear helmets.

Teams consist of ten players each: a goalie, three defensive players, three midfielders and three attackmen. The object of the game is to get the ball into the opponents' goal with the crosses. The team with the most goals at the end of the game wins. The goalie guards the goal, and the defensive players stay near the goalie to help protect the area.

The midfielders can go anywhere on the field. The attackmen are usually the players who score the goals.

The game starts with a face-off between two players at the center of the field to see which team gets the ball first. Players then use their crosses to pass the ball to team members, trying to get the ball into the opponents' goal. The opposing team can take the ball by using the end of their crosse to try and knock the ball out of the net of another player's crosse. Only the goalies can touch the ball with their hands. Players can use their bodies to bump other players to try to get the ball. This is called *body checking*, and it is only allowed above the waist and below the shoulders.

Men and women play lacrosse, but the rules are slightly different for men's and women's teams. For example, the women wear less protective gear and body checking is not allowed. Rules also differ depending on if the team is a youth team, a college team or a professional team.

---

b Read the text again. Mark the statements *T* (true) or *F* (false).

1 Lacrosse is played inside. — *F*
2 The lacrosse sticks can be different sizes. ☐
3 The object of the game is to catch the ball with the crosse. ☐
4 Defensive players cannot touch the ball with their hands. ☐
5 Body checking is against the rules in men's games. ☐
6 The rules are different depending on the type of team. ☐

c Read the text again and answer the questions.

1 What equipment is used in lacrosse?
2 How big is the lacrosse field without the goals?
3 How many players are on each team?
4 What do the different players do?
5 What is one way women's lacrosse is different from men's lacrosse?

Skills in mind

6 Listen

a Look at the pictures. What are the sports? Write down any words you know associated with these sports.

A ....

B ....

C ....
....

D ....
....

E ....
....

F ....
....

b ▶ **CD4 T07** Listen to these five short sports commentaries. Match the correct sport with each speaker. Write 1–5 in the boxes. There is one photo you won't use.

c Now write the words you heard that helped you choose each answer.

1 ....
2 ....
3 ....
4 ....
5 ....

EXAM TIP

Matching opinions with pictures

In this type of task, you hear five short extracts that have a common theme.

- Before you start listening, look at all the information you have already.
- Think of everything you know about the subject and try to predict the words the speaker will use.
- Try to choose the answers during the first listening and check them during the second one.
- Some of the vocabulary can be difficult. Don't worry if you don't understand every word; just try to understand the general meaning.

Unit check

1 Fill in the blanks

Complete the text with the words in the box.

| that | what | when | where | which | which | ~~who~~ | who | whose | why |

Edson Barboza and Luiz Cane, _____who_____ are martial arts fighters, both fought other competitors in March 2011. The fights were in Newark, ¹_____ is in New Jersey in the United States. This competition wasn't just to see ²_____ was the best. It was also a competition ³_____ raised money for charity. The fighters raised money for Nova Friburgo, Brazil, ⁴_____ a terrible storm damaged the city. Both fighters had a good reason ⁵_____ they wanted to raise money for this city. Barboza is from Nova Friburgo, but he wasn't there ⁶_____ the storm happened. Barboza, ⁷_____ family still lives in Nova Friburgo, said his wife's parents lost a lot of their things because of the storm. Cane also knows a lot of people in Nova Friburgo and wanted to help. Barboza beat Anthony Njokuani, and Cane beat Eliot Marshall, but ⁸_____ really matters is how much money they raised for charity, ⁹_____ was over $20,000.

| | 9 |

2 Choose the correct answers

Circle the correct answer: a, b or c.

1 The man _____ I met is from Chile.
   a which   b whose   c (who)

2 She didn't pass the exam, _____ means she has to repeat the year.
   a which   b what   c that

3 The person _____ lent me that DVD wants it back.
   a which   b whose   c who

4 The book _____ you ordered has arrived.
   a that   b it   c what

5 I don't understand _____ he's saying.
   a which   b that   c what

6 They couldn't give us the information _____ we needed.
   a it   b that   c what

7 _____ they need is a new director.
   a Who   b That   c What

8 The field _____ we played the game on was really wet.
   a who   b that   c what

9 The boy _____ dog bit you apologized.
   a whose   b who   c which

| | 8 |

3 Vocabulary

Underline the correct words.

1 One of the two boxers fell out of the ring / court.

2 He played really well, and he scored / won the last goal, too.

3 Make sure you wear your gloves / helmet. You don't want to hurt your head.

4 It was an exciting game. In the end, we tied / beat 2–2.

5 The referee ejected / beat him from the game.

6 I'm sure that we're going to win / beat the next team we play.

7 I wanted to go swimming, but I forgot to take my racket / goggles, so I couldn't.

8 The field / rink we played on was in bad condition. It had almost no grass on it at all.

9 The waves were too rough to go surfing / boxing.

| | 8 |

How did you do?

Total: | 25 |

| 😊 Very good 25 – 20 | 😐 OK 19 – 16 | 😞 Review Unit 3 again 15 or less |

4 People are people.

1 Grammar

★ what clauses

a ▶ CD4 T08 Listen to the embarrassing stories A–D. Write the correct letter beside the quote that matches it.

1 "What was really embarrassing was that it took a couple of days for the color to wash off." ☐

2 "What was even worse was that I had to sing it all over again." ☐

3 "What annoyed me the most was my dad's reaction! I'll never forgive him." ☐

4 "What made me feel bad was that the teacher had a bump on his head for the next week." ☐

b There is an extra word in some of these sentences. ~~Cross out~~ the extra word or write a check (✓) if the sentence is correct.

1 This is what I like ~~that~~ best about the job. ......

2 What annoys me is about Josie is that she's always talking. ......

3 What you see is what you get. ......

4 What I need to concentrate on that is grammar. ......

5 I like what thing she says about the class. ......

6 It doesn't matter what you say, she never listens. ......

c Join the two sentences to make one sentence using *what*.

1 Anne is always late. It annoys me.

   What annoys me about Anne is that she is always late.

2 John always changes his mind. It's very frustrating.

   ......

3 She argues a lot with her sister. It makes life difficult for her parents.

   ......

4 The teachers ask you to do things. It's essential to do them.

   ......

5 That restaurant has a good atmosphere. This makes it special.

   ......

6 You should do certain things when people are hurt. It's good to know them.

   ......

2 Pronunciation

★ Sentence stress and rhythm

a ▶ CD4 T09 Listen and underline the stressed words.

1 What I <u>really</u> want to do is take a <u>nap</u>.
2 I never listen to what he says.
3 What really impressed me was her presentation.
4 I never know what to say in these situations.
5 What I'd like to know is where we are all going to stay.
6 This isn't what you were saying last week.

b ▶ CD4 T09 Listen again and repeat.

3 Vocabulary

★ Personality

a Match the descriptions 1–6 with the adjectives a–f.

1 someone who is caring and understanding   a bubbly

2 someone who is superficial   b smug

3 someone who is silly and forgetful   c shallow

4 someone who is clever and funny   d sympathetic

5 someone who is very pleased with him or herself   e witty

6 someone who is happy and full of energy   f scatterbrained

b Which person do the descriptions refer to? Write the letters a–d.

(A) Sorry, no eating in class!

(B) Oops!

(C) Katie, you look great! What's your secret?

(D) My father always says that what counts is who you know...

1 Ralph is so pretentious. He's always talking about famous people that he's met and pretending he's important. ....

2 He's so hypocritical! ....

3 Carl is so careless. He never looks where he's going! ....

4 I love hanging out with Mike. He's so charming. He always makes me feel good. ....

c Complete the sentences with the words in the box.

> pushy   ~~intellectual~~   smug   shallow   sympathetic   cheeky

1 Walter loves learning and thinking. He's really __*intellectual*__ .

2 Don't be _____ . It's not nice to answer back to people.

3 Be careful. She's very _____ . She'll try to get you to do what she wants.

4 Rachel's very _____ these days. She always acts so pleased with herself.

5 The teacher was very _____ when she heard my bag had been stolen.

6 Don't expect her to understand if you have a problem. She's pretty _____ .

d (Vocabulary bank) Complete the crossword.

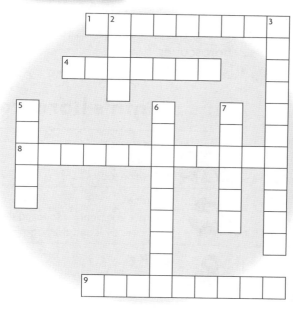

Across

1 James is so _____ ! He does the craziest things.

4 Don't be _____ ! Let other people have a turn.

8 She seems a little pushy, but in fact she's very _____ when you get to know her.

9 He lent me his bike and walked home! What an _____ thing to do.

Down

2 She never gets too excited. She's a very _____ person.

3 You drank all the milk and there's nothing left for us! That's not very _____ , is it?

5 He never understands anything because he's not very _____ .

6 He's always jumping up and down and laughing. He's a very _____ person.

7 Don't look so sad. You need to be a bit more _____ about things.

4 Grammar

✳ Verbs + gerund/infinitive review

a (Circle) the correct words to complete the horoscopes.

this month's horoscope ...

 Aquarius
You'll enjoy *to be* / (*being*) the center of attention today.

 Pisces
Try not *to repeat* / *repeating* the same mistakes over and over again.

 Aries
You can't stand *to follow* / *following* the crowd. Today is no exception.

 Taurus
Have you borrowed any money from anyone recently? Remember *to pay* / *paying* them back today or you could get into trouble.

 Gemini
Don't stop *to believe* / *believing* in yourself, and you'll get what you want.

 Cancer
Don't refuse *to meet* / *meeting* a friend today. He or she could be important for your future.

 Leo
Don't stop *to talk* / *talking* to a stranger you'll meet today. They'll waste your time.

 Virgo
Can you remember ever *to feel* / *feeling* so happy? Make the most of this special time!

 Libra
It's time you stopped *to think* / *thinking* about the past. You need to live in the present.

 Scorpio
You enjoy *to be* / *being* outdoors. Take time off work and go for a walk.

 Sagittarius
Take time to stop *to think* / *thinking* about what's going on around you. You might miss something important if you don't.

 Capricorn
Try not *to lose* / *losing* your temper with a friend or someone in your family. You'll be glad you made the effort.

b Complete the dialogue with the correct form of the verbs in parentheses.

Dave: What took you so long?

Jane: I stopped ___*to buy*___ (buy) some food on the way.

Dave: Oh good! Did you remember
¹ _____ (get) some milk?

Jane: Yes! Guess who I met at the supermarket ... Sally Watson!

Dave: Sally Watson? I remember
² _____ (be) friends with her. In fact, we used to hang out with each other when we were about 18.

Jane: Really? Why did you stop
³ _____ (hang out) with her?

Dave: We were just different. I enjoyed
⁴ _____ (go) to parties and
⁵ _____ (meet) people. She couldn't stand ⁶ _____ (hang around) with my friends. I haven't heard from her in ages.

Jane: Well, she was asking about you. She gave me her new phone number.

Dave: Really?

Jane: Yeah, here it is. Don't forget
⁷ _____ (call) her! It sounds like she wants to hang out again.

5 Everyday English

a Complete each expression with one word.

1 I could _____ without ...

2 Look _____ .

3 _____ way!

4 I'd _____ thought ...

5 ... and _____ on.

6 Don't look _____ me.

b Complete the dialogues with the expressions from Exercise 5a.

1 A: Hey – someone's eaten all the chocolate!

   B: Well, _____ . I don't even like chocolate very much.

2 A: Do you think we'll win the game on Sunday?

   B: _____ ! They're a much, much better team than we are.

3 A: What kind of books does he like?

   B: Oh, you know – thrillers, detective stories, police novels _____ .

4 A: Hey – _____ . You're in my way.

   B: Oh, sorry. I didn't know you were trying to get by.

5 A: Let me give you some advice.

   B: No, _____ it, thanks. The last time I took your advice, things got worse!

6 A: Mr. Anderson really helped me with my problem.

   B: Really? _____ he would be unapproachable.

6 Study help

✱ Using a range of vocabulary when writing

- One way of improving your writing skills is to avoid repeating yourself by using an appropriate range of vocabulary. This is particularly important when writing a story or an essay.

- Before you start writing, think of key words that you will use, and then write down synonyms for them. You can also write adjectives or nouns that you associate with the key words.

- When you have finished, reread your text and find alternatives for repeated words or phrases. You can use the words from your list. Use a dictionary to check the exact meaning of the synonyms.

Match the underlined words with their meanings a–d.

1 NBA2K11 is one of the hottest video games right now. Everyone is playing it.

2 The *Harry Potter* craze has made reading very popular with young people and has helped bookstores increase their sales.

3 Last year's fashion fad, wearing colorful braces on your teeth, has passed. What's going to replace it?

4 When something is in fashion, it's popular and lots of people want to buy or have it.

a a passing trend or one that lasts for a short time

b a trend that is followed with great enthusiasm

c the current trend

d latest and most exciting

Skills in mind

7 Write a story

a Read these two texts. Do they contain the same information?

Text 1

He opened the door. The room was dark and messy. He turned on the light. The room was bigger than it seemed. There were books everywhere. Bookshelves were on the walls, and there were books on the table and on the chairs. Books covered the floor.

John panicked. He would never find the book he was looking for.

Text 2

Slowly he turned the key in the door. His hand was shaking, but, carefully, he pushed the door open. The heavy curtains were drawn, and it was dark and gloomy inside.

It was obvious, even in the dim light, that no one had been in here for a long time. He stepped in and almost fell over a mountain of books on the floor. The room was a complete mess. There were books everywhere. Old books were packed into the bookshelves that lined the walls of the room. Every surface was covered with books and papers. Dictionaries and reference books were lying all over the center table. He took one of these books from the table and turned towards a chair. It was also covered with books of every kind: atlases, novels and dictionaries in languages he didn't recognize.

Everywhere he looked there were books. Where had they all come from? And where was the cozy library that he used to go in as a young boy? Where had it disappeared to?

John felt his heart fill with fear and panic. How was he going to find his mother's diary among all these books? Would he ever find out the truth about what happened that night?

b Read the two texts again and answer the questions.

1 What is the difference between the texts?

2 What does the descriptive language in Text 2 tell us about John?

3 What does the descriptive language in Text 2 tell us about the room?

4 Do you think that John has been in the room before?

5 Why do you think he is looking for his mother's diary?

c Now continue the story.

Then, suddenly, he saw it on the table beside his mother's favorite chair. Of course... He was shaking as he walked over and picked it up, holding his breath as he turned to the first entry.

EXAM TIP

Writing a story

- Don't start writing immediately, but first spend a few minutes writing down your ideas.
- List the characters and make notes on their appearance and personality.
- Decide where they live and the important events in their lives, and choose adjectives to describe them.
- Think of where the story takes place and the atmosphere. Try to imagine yourself there. How would you feel?
- Now decide what action happens.
- Always remember to check your story for spelling, grammar and punctuation mistakes.

Unit check

1 Fill in the blanks

Complete the text with the words in the box.

| being   pretentious   what   calm   famous   to be   ~~shy~~   witty   whenever   tried to |

The English novelist Jane Austen was born in 1775. She was _____shy_____ as a child and didn't enjoy
[1] _____ in the spotlight. Austen's life was pretty [2] _____ and without great excitment
or change. She was educated at home by her father, and [3] _____ she liked best was reading and
writing. She didn't want [4] _____ noticed, so she kept her writing a secret and wrote on small
pieces of paper which she hid [5] _____ anyone came into the room. Her father supported her
and [6] _____ find a publisher for her. Her novels are [7] _____ for making fun of anyone
who is smug or selfish. In her writing, she is very critical of [8] _____ people, and her heroines are
always intelligent as well as [9] _____ and attractive.

| **9** |

2 Choose the correct answers

Circle the correct answer: a, b or c.

1 I _____ my roommate at a party.
   a knew   b (met)   c made

2 Karl has a terrible _____ of humor.
   a sensitive   b mood   c sense

3 Did you enjoy _____ to her?
   a talk   b talking   c to talk

4 Sally refused _____ at the conference.
   a speak   b speaking   c to speak

5 Don't go near Stuart. He's in a really bad _____ .
   a mood   b nature   c sense

6 I've _____ her since I was in grade school.
   a found   b met   c known

7 Tell Anne about your problem. She's
   very _____ .
   a sympathetic   b smug   c witty

8 I can't stand _____ this any longer.
   a do   b doing   c to do

9 Please, try _____ . There was nothing else
   I could do.
   a understand   b to understand
   c understanding

| **8** |

3 Vocabulary

Underline the correct words.

1 Someone who is intelligent is _smart_ / cheeky / scatterbrained.
2 Someone who listens and cares is smug / careless / sympathetic.
3 Someone who doesn't get too excited is excitable / calm / bubbly.
4 Someone who always tries to get what they want is pushy / shallow / cheeky.
5 Someone who takes a positive view of things is intellectual / upbeat / careless.
6 Someone who does unusual things is unapproachable / pretentious / eccentric.
7 Someone who forgets things easily is scatterbrained / pushy / witty.
8 Someone you can go and talk to is unselfish / approachable / upbeat.
9 Someone who talks back to people is shallow / cheeky / selfish.

| **8** |

How did you do?

Total: | 25 |

 Very good
25 – 20

 OK
19 – 16

 Review Unit 4 again
15 or less

5 Time travelers

1 Grammar

✱ Reported speech review

a Match the two parts of the sentences in each group.

1 Caroline told Sara   _b_   a   Sara that Caroline was making a mistake.

2 Sara said, ...   b   that she was going to move to Canada.

3 Marco told   c   "I'm going to miss you."

4 John said   ....   d   that Russian was pretty difficult.

   e   to me that he wanted to study Russian next year.

5 The teacher told   ....

   f   him he would have to learn the Russian alphabet before he started.

6 I told him   ....

7 My dad told   ....   g   him that I was scared of horses.

   h   me he wanted to take me horseback riding this weekend.

8 He said   ....

   i   he had booked us a lesson at 11 o'clock on Saturday.

9 I told   ....

b ⟨Circle⟩ the correct words in the second sentence.

1 She told me that she couldn't come to the meeting.

"I ⟨can't⟩ / couldn't come to the meeting."

2 He told me to call him if I needed help.
"You call / Call me if you need help."

3 The teacher asked her if she had given the letter to her parents.

"Did you give / Would you give the letter to your parents?"

4 He said he would come over to see her the following day.

"I'd come over / I'll come over to see you tomorrow."

5 Steven said he had seen Mark the previous day.
"I've seen / I saw Mark yesterday."

6 He told me that he was going out with Susana that evening.

"I go out / I'm going out with Susana this evening."

c Rewrite these sentences using direct speech.

1 He asked me if I had seen the latest Harry Potter movie.

Have you seen the latest Harry Potter movie?
....

2 I replied that I hadn't but that I was reading the book.

....

3 He asked me if I would lend him the book when I had finished with it.

....

4 I asked him what he knew about the author.

....

5 He told me that the author, J. K. Rowling, had always wanted to write books.

....

2 Vocabulary

✱ Expressions with *time*

a Look at the cartoon and read the joke. Check (✓) the funniest answer 1, 2 or 3.

Q: What time was it when the elephant sat on the clock?

A: ....

1 I don't know. ☐

2 Two o'clock? ☐

3 Time to get a new clock! ☐

b Complete the sentences with the correct tense of the verbs in the box.

give spend take waste

1 There was no deadline on the project, so we .... our time.

2 I hate visiting my brother. He always .... me a hard time about my job.

3 He's really fit. He .... most of his free time at the gym.

4 So far this evening, you .... a lot of time watching TV. Do some homework!

c Circle the correct preposition.

1 I'm taking some time *off / on* work to redecorate the house.

2 I called just *at / in* time to get the last tickets.

3 The new teacher never arrives *at / on* time.

4 We didn't get to finish painting because we ran *off / out* of time.

d Complete the sentences with the word in **bold** at the end. You will need to use more than one word.

1 Don't __*waste time*__ during the exam. (**waste**)

2 He's taking some .... because he's been working hard lately. (**off**)

3 You can .... because the train doesn't leave until six. (**take**)

4 I don't think I passed the test. I ...., and I didn't answer all the questions. (**ran**)

5 She arrived .... to see him. (**just**)

e [Vocabulary bank] Complete the sentences with the words in the box.

of all   to kill   to lose   a matter of
up   ~~of my life~~   from

1 I had the time __*of my life*__ in Miami.

2 Who do you think is the best rock singer .... time?

3 My mother travels to the United States .... time to time.

4 Hurry up! There's no time ....!

5 One day we'll win the championship, I'm sure. It's just .... time.

6 Time's .... Please hand in your tests.

7 The play doesn't start for another two hours, so we have a lot of time ....

3 Pronunciation

✱ The schwa /ə/

a ▶ CD4 T10 Listen to the sentences. <u>Underline</u> the unstressed syllables with the schwa /ə/ sound.

1 I don't have <u>a</u> lot <u>of</u> time.

2 He wastes a lot of time on the phone.

3 He arrived just in time to have breakfast with us.

4 You can take some time off next week when we're not so busy.

5 Do you have time for a cup of tea?

b ▶ CD4 T10 Listen again and repeat.

4 Grammar

★ Reporting verbs review

a | Match the two parts of the sentences. Write the letters a–h on the blanks.

1 Cathy reminded her father ...g... a her to stay in school.

2 In the conversation he had persuaded .... b she was worried about him.

3 She said that .... c over-worked and stressed people to relax.

4 And she advised .... d a book to him.

5 She recommended .... e to think about her advice.

6 The book encourages .... f that they learn to do things more slowly.

7 It also suggests .... g about a conversation they had when she was fifteen.

8 Cathy asked her dad to promise .... h him to stop working so hard.

b | ▶ CD4 T11 Cathy calls her father. Listen and (circle) the correct words to complete the statements.

1 Cathy calls her father and asks if he has (received) / sent her email.

2 He says that he *got / sent* it a week ago.

3 He says he *didn't read it / didn't read it carefully*.

4 Cathy tells him to *take time off / work hard*.

5 At first, her father *refuses / wants* to listen to her.

6 He promises to *read the email / take time off* once they have finished the phone call.

c | Rewrite the sentences so they have the same meaning. Use the verb in **bold** at the end.

1 "I'll be on time tomorrow morning!" **(promise)**

   He promised that he would be on time the next morning.

2 "You should buy the latest Coldplay album." **(recommend)**

   Laura _____ .

3 "Don't ever do that again!" **(warn)**

   Their mom _____ .

4 "Let's go to the movies on Friday." **(suggest)**

   She _____ .

5 "I wouldn't buy that cell phone." **(advise)**

   Jane _____ .

6 "If you join our gym you'll be fit in just a month." **(claim)**

   The instructor _____ .

7 "I didn't break the vase." **(deny)**

   She _____ .

8 "I won't accept homework that isn't done on time." **(say)**

   The teacher _____ .

Fiction in mind

a Read this extract from H. G. Wells's *The Time Machine*. Circle the word a, b or c that is closest in meaning to the words numbered 1–8 in the text.

The time traveler is thousands of years in the future. He has stopped the machine to look at the world around him.

The machine was standing on a sloping beach. The ocean stretched away to the southwest, rising into a sharp bright horizon against the ¹wan sky. There were no waves, because there wasn't a breath of wind. Only a slight oily swell rose and fell like a gentle breathing, and showed that the ocean was still moving and alive. And along the water's edge was a thick layer of salt, that was pink under the ²lurid sky. There was a sense of oppression in my head, and I noticed that I was breathing very fast. The sensation reminded me of my only experience of mountaineering, and from that I realized that the air was ³more rarefied than it is in our times.

Far away, up the desolate slope, I heard a ⁴harsh scream, and saw something like a huge white butterfly go flying up into the sky and then, circling, it disappeared over some low ⁵hillocks in the distance. The sound of its voice was so ⁶dismal that I shivered and sat more firmly on the machine. Looking around me again, I saw that, quite near, what I had thought was a reddish piece of rock was moving slowly toward me. Then I saw that it was really a monstrous crab-like creature. Can you imagine a crab as large as a table, with its legs moving slowly and uncertainly, its big claws ⁷swaying, its long antennae, like whips, waving and feeling, and its eyes ⁸gleaming at you on either side of its metallic front? I could see the feelers in its mouth moving around as it came toward me.

1 a wet   b (pale) c closed
2 a curious   b delicious   c brightly colored
3 a thinner   b more delicious   c lower
4 a black   b funny   c unpleasantly strong
5 a small birds   b small rivers   c small hills
6 a very sad   b very happy   c very quiet
7 a walking very quickly   b moving from side to side
   c shouting loudly
8 a shining brightly   b laughing   c closing

b Read the text again and answer the questions.

1 How did the traveler know that the ocean was still alive?

   ----

2 How did the traveler know that the air in the future was thinner?

   ----

3 Why did the traveler sit "more firmly on the machine"?

   ----

4 What did the traveler think the crab-like creature was, at first?

READING TIP

Getting the general meaning

● When you're reading, don't worry if you don't understand the exact meaning of every word. Try not to stop when you are unsure. Keep reading and see if you can get the general meaning.

● Once you have a general idea of what the text means, read it again, using a dictionary to help you with more difficult words.

Skills in mind

6 Read

a Read this extract from the *Hitchhiker's Guide to the Galaxy* by Douglas Adams quickly. Is it about the past, the present or the future? Give reasons for your answer.

It is an important and popular fact that things are not always what they seem. For instance, on the planet Earth, man had always assumed that he was more intelligent than dolphins because he had achieved so much – the wheel, New York, wars and so on – while all the dolphins had ever done was muck about in the water having a good time. But [1] conversely, the dolphins had always believed they were far more intelligent than man – for precisely the same reasons.

Curiously enough, the dolphins had long known of the impending destruction of the planet Earth, and had made many attempts to alert mankind to the danger; but most of their communications were misinterpreted as amusing attempts to punch soccer balls or whistle for [2] tidbits, so they eventually gave up and left the Earth shortly before the Vogons arrived.

The last ever dolphin message was misinterpreted as a surprisingly [3] sophisticated attempt to do a double-backwards somersault through a hoop while whistling The Star-Spangled Banner, but in fact the message was this: So long, and thanks for all the fish.

In fact there was only one species on the planet more intelligent than dolphins, and they spent a lot of time in research laboratories running around inside wheels and conducting frighteningly [4] elegant and [5] subtle experiments on man. The fact that once again man completely [6] misinterpreted this relationship was entirely according to these creatures' plans.

b Match the words in the text 1–6 with the definitions a–f.

a   small pieces of food   ....
b   on the other hand   ....
c   understood something different ....
d   clever and complicated   ....
e   graceful and attractive   ....
f   clever but not obvious   ....

c Choose the correct answer: a, b or c.

1   Why did man think he was more intelligent than dolphins?
   a   Because man didn't understand dolphins.
   b   Because man thought he had achieved more than dolphins.
   c   Because New York was an important city.

2   What does "muck about" mean?
   a   Swim.   b   Perform tricks.   c   Play.

3   What did the dolphins know that man didn't?
   a   That the planet Earth was going to be destroyed.
   b   That *The Star-Spangled Banner* had a secret meaning.
   c   That the Vogons liked fish.

4   What was "entirely according to these creatures' plans"?
   a   That they spent a long time in labs.
   b   That man did not understand what they were really doing.
   c   That they were more intelligent than dolphins.

EXAM TIP

Multiple choice
- Skim through the text to get a general idea of its meaning.
- Read the questions carefully before reading the text again.
- If you are unsure, eliminate any obviously incorrect answers first. When you choose an answer, try to find a logical reason for your choice.

Unit check

1 Fill in the blanks

Complete the text with the words in the box.

> has promised   time   that   asked   on   spent   ~~last~~   warned   denied   having

This is a report from _____last_____ Friday's Student Council meeting. Everyone arrived [1]_____ time. The chairperson, Pete, [2]_____ everyone to give their opinion on the quality of the food in the school cafeteria. Caroline said [3]_____ she thought the meals were pretty good. She also suggested [4]_____ more vegetarian and organic meals. Karl [5]_____ that organic food in particular would be more expensive. Jonathan said they had [6]_____ enough time talking about organic food during the last meeting. Pete asked Jonathan not to waste [7]_____ arguing with the others, and Jonathan left. Some people claimed that insects had been found in some meals recently, but a representative from the cafeteria [8]_____ this. Pete wrote a report and the principal [9]_____ to read it as soon as possible.

> 9

2 Choose the correct answers

Circle the correct answer: a, b or c.

1 Catherine asked us _____ our opinions on the play.
   a give   b (to give)   c giving

2 She denied _____ about the letter.
   a knowing   b to know   c know

3 He convinced her _____ it.
   a doing   b to do   c do

4 The teacher warned us _____ it.
   a not doing   b not to do   c to don't

5 He said that he _____ I would be happy.
   a hoping   b is hoping   c hoped

6 She _____ Angela all about her vacation.
   a said   b told   c told to

7 She promised _____ the next time she was in the area.
   a calling   b that she call   c to call

8 I decided _____ anything about the misunderstanding.
   a not saying   b not to say   c not that I say

9 He told _____ that he had tickets for the concert.
   a to me   b I   c me

> 8

3 Vocabulary

Complete the sentences. Write one word in each space.

1 I _____spend_____ a lot of time every day on the Internet.

2 That's a really ridiculous question. Please don't _____ my time.

3 He was really tired, so he took some time _____ work and went on vacation.

4 I think Rafael Nadal is the best tennis player of _____ time.

5 The party was fantastic! I had the time of my _____ .

6 If I get home late, my parents always _____ me a hard time.

7 Hurry up! We're running _____ of time!

8 We were almost late, but we got there just _____ time to catch the bus.

9 There's no hurry. We can _____ our time.

> 8

How did you do?

Total: | 25

| :) Very good 25 – 20 | :\| OK 19 – 16 | :(Review Unit 5 again 15 or less |

6 In and out of fashion

1 Grammar

✳ used to and would

a Check (✓) the sentences if you can replace *used to* with *would*.

1 During our vacations we used to play outside until it was dark. ✓

2 My dad used to whistle while he was working. ☐

3 The dog used to follow her everywhere. ☐

4 They used to arrive at the end of June and stay until September. ☐

5 She used to have green hair. ☐

6 I used to have a horse, but I sold it. ☐

b Complete the table with information about what we do now.

then		now
1	sent telegrams	*send emails*
2	used candles	
3	made their own toys	
4	traveled in carriages	
5	wrote letters	
6	wore long skirts and dresses	
7	listened to records	
8	had a lot of children	

c Write sentences using the information in the table.

1 *In the past, people used to send telegrams, now they send emails.*

2 _____

3 _____

4 _____

5 _____

6 _____

7 _____

8 _____

d Complete the sentences with the verbs in the box. Use *would* where you can or *used to*.

spend   not go   drive   find
be   ~~want~~

1 I _used to want_ to be a teacher, but now I think I'll be a doctor.

2 They _____ hours playing cards every evening.

3 I _____ languages pretty difficult, but now I speak Italian and Russian fluently.

4 You're a successful businesswoman now. It's hard to believe you _____ a rebellious child.

5 When I was a kid I _____ anywhere without my dog.

6 He _____ a Ford. Now he has a BMW.

32   UNIT 6

2 Vocabulary

✱ In and out of fashion

Complete the article about popular sunglasses from 1960 to today. Use the words in the box.

> addictive   all the rage   ~~caught on~~   craze   eagerly   in   heyday   the latest

In the 1960s, teashades were popular. John Lennon, the Beatles singer, wore teashades, and the trend ___caught on___ .

In the 1970s, sunglasses that changed color were popular. They changed in different lights. People put their sunglasses on, went outside and ¹ _____ waited for them to change.

Oversized sunglasses were the ² _____ in the 1980s. Singer Elton John and other celebrities made these glasses popular. Movie star Tom Cruise was in his ³ _____ in the 1980s. He wore aviator glasses in two popular movies, and other people started wearing them, too.

In the 1990s, wrap sunglasses were popular. They wrapped around the head. Athletes liked them because you could wear them playing sports. They were ⁴ _____ with other people because they looked futuristic.

After 2000, wearing oversized sunglasses became an ⁵ _____ phase for many celebrities. The bigger the better! Celebrities often weren't seen in public without their large sunglasses on – even indoors.

What's ⁶ _____ style of sunglasses? Big sunglasses are still ⁷ _____ , but now they are flashier.

3 Vocabulary

✱ Adverbs and adverbial phrases

a Join the two sentences to make one, using adverbial phrases. There is sometimes more than one possibility.

1 He looked at me. He seemed surprised.

   He looked at me with surprise.

2 The dog barked at us. It sounded horrible.

   _____

3 He teaches English. His way of teaching is fun.

   _____

4 They listened to her. They were enthusiastic.

   _____

5 We found the house. It was difficult to find.

   _____

6 He said hello to me. He was friendly.

   _____

7 We need to do this again. We need to do something different.

   _____

8 The children waited for the clown to arrive. They were excited.

   _____

b (Circle) the correct adverbial phrase to complete the sentences.

You might be told it's wrong to look at people ¹ (in a rude way) / in a surprising way, but a new craze called Stare Master makes it OK. People are lining up ² with difficulty / with enthusiasm to take part in staring contests. The Stare Master contests have really strict rules. You aren't allowed to laugh, close your eyes, nod or move. Some people enter the contest ³ with fear / with excitement, but most are excited. "It's great," said one fan, "because it tests your self-control ⁴ in a different way / in a horrible way." It was invented by two friends because they were bored and wanted to spend their free time in ⁵ a fun way / a friendly way.

4 Vocabulary

✳ Common adverbial phrases

a Circle the correct adverbial phrase.

1 She's the first person to be voted chairperson three years *in public / (in a row)*.

2 They held the meeting *on purpose / in private*, and no one knew anything about it.

3 Can you call a taxi for me? I'm *in a hurry / in a row* to get to the train station.

4 Please don't tell anyone. I was told *on purpose / in secret*.

5 Can you help Janet? She's *in a panic / in a hurry* about the exam.

6 I don't like talking *in public / in private*. Crowds make me nervous.

7 I think he said it *by accident / on purpose* to make everyone laugh.

8 Don't be angry. She did it *by accident / on purpose*. It's not like her to cause problems.

b Complete the puzzle. Use the mystery word to complete the last sentence.

1 When you do things in front of other people, you do them in _____ .

2 When you have to do something quickly you're in a _____ .

3 When you don't want everyone to see what you're doing, you do it in _____ .

4 If you worry and get anxious about something, you are in a ____ *panic* ____ .

5 If you do the same thing lots of times, you do it several times in a _____ .

6 If you hide something from other people, you do it in _____ .

7 If you don't mean to do something, you do it by _____ .

8 When you do something on _____ , you mean to do it.

c **Vocabulary bank** Complete the sentences with the words in the box.

backward   out   down   ~~bottom~~   wrong   toe

1 The house was really dirty, so we cleaned it from top to ____ *bottom* ____ .

2 Your sweater looks kind of strange. I think it's inside _____ .

3 Sorry, that's not right. You plugged it in the _____ way.

4 You have your T-shirt on _____ .

5 He was covered in mud from head to _____ .

6 Turn the bottle upside _____ and shake it. Then the sauce will come out.

5 Pronunciation

✳ /æ/ s*a*t and /ɛ/ s*e*t

a ▶ CD4 T12 Listen and circle the correct word.

1 He lost his *(bat) / bet*.

2 Do you have my *pan / pen*?

3 It's *Dad / dead*!

4 There's a *band / bend* in the road.

5 The cat *sat / set* by the fire.

6 The *man / men* can stay.

b ▶ CD4 T12 Listen and repeat.

6 Read

a
Read the text. Complete the sentences with one word in each blank. There is often more than one possibility.

Fashion & music

We're used to seeing music stars like Madonna and Lady Gaga wear fashions that _____create_____ an image for them. But music and fashion have always been closely linked. The tough, leather-wearing image of early rock stars [1] _____ Gene Vincent influenced a generation of young people in Europe and in the United States. A cultural war [2] _____ out in the mid-1960s in the UK over the rivalry between the "Mods" (who favored high-fashion, expensive styles) and the "Rockers" (who wore T-shirts and leather). Followers of each style had their favorite musical groups, who fed into the rivalry by releasing records praising one style and criticizing the other. In the 1960s, the Beatles brought mop-top haircuts, collarless blazers and Beatle boots into fashion.

Rock musicians were among the first people to wear hippie clothing and introduced such styles as the Nehru jacket. Bands like the Beatles wore custom-made clothes that had a strong [3] _____ on 1960s style. As rock music genres developed, what an artist wore became as [4] _____ as the music itself in defining the artist's intent and relationship to the audience. The glam rock of the 1970s brought fashion to a new [5] _____ of importance in rock music with the "glitter" image of artists like the New York Dolls. Some artists who had been active in the late 1960s, such as David Bowie, also adopted a glam-influenced look.

In the late 1970s, disco groups helped make flashy urban styles fashionable, while new wave groups started wearing conservative [6] _____ including suit jackets and thin ties, in an [7] _____ to be as different from mainstream rockers as possible.

In the early 1990s, the popularity of grunge brought in a fashion of its own. Grunge musicians and fans wore torn jeans, old shoes, flannel shirts and backward baseball hats, and they grew their hair against the clean-cut image that was popular at the [8] _____ , together with a heavily commercialized pop music culture. Musicians continue to be fashion icons. Pop-culture magazines such as *Rolling Stone* often [9] _____ fashion sections featuring musicians as models.

b
▶ CD4 T13 Listen to the radio call-in show. Four people talk about their favorite songs about fashion. Complete the chart with the names in the box.

> "Vogue"   The Kinks   George Michael   "Freedom"
> "Dedicated Follower of Fashion"   Madonna   David Bowie   "Fashion"

Speaker	Song name	Artist
Janine		
Andy		
Patricia		
Mark		

7 Listen

a ▶ CD4 T14 Listen to the radio show host introduce Philippa Chandler. Make notes about who she is and what she does.

b Answer *T* (true), *F* (false) or *D* (doesn't say) below.

1 Philippa Chandler is a radio show host. ☐

2 *The People Show* features fashionable people. ☐

3 Next Big Thing is a company that predicts new trends. ☐

c ▶ CD4 T14 Before you listen again, circle the best answer, a, b or c, to complete the sentences below. Then listen to check.

1 Philippa's job is to
  a write about new trends.
  b start new trends.
  c help her clients create new trends.

2 A regular part of Philippa's work is to
  a drink coffee.
  b go to popular surf resorts.
  c conduct surveys.

3 Philippa found out about her current job
  a thanks to a newspaper article.
  b from a friend.
  c through a freelance job agency.

4 Philippa believed she was perfect for the job because …
  a she loved coffee and surfing the net.
  b she is sociable and had done research on why people buy things.
  c she is curious and likes asking people questions.

d Answer the questions. You may need to listen again.

1 Explain, in your own words, what is meant by the "next big thing."

....

....

2 Why are Philippa's clients interested in the information she collects?

....

....

3 When is Philippa's research not productive?

....

....

4 What advice does Philippa give young people looking for a job?

....

....

EXAM TIP

Question types in listening

- Before you start, read the questions thoroughly and make sure you understand them. Underline key words and try to predict what you will hear.

- There may be different types of questions. In Exercise 7, there are three question types.

  Type 1 You decide if the statement is true or false or if you don't have enough information to answer it.

  Type 2 You decide which answer completes the phrase best. Remember in this type, you may hear all the phrases given, but only one is relevant to the question.

  Type 3 You answer the questions, usually with a short or complete sentence. Always check your spelling, grammar and punctuation.

Unit check

1 Fill in the blanks

Complete the text with the words in the box.

popular   craze   are concerned   ~~young~~   potentially   excitement   wasting   fear   sharing   group

Bebo is one of the hottest websites among _____*young*_____ people. It's aimed at people age 13–30. It's the most [1] _____ with students. Bebo allows you to chat with your friends, [2] _____ space on the Web together. "There is a huge demand for this type of service," says Bebo's founder, Michael Birch with [3] _____ . When you join Bebo, you choose a school or college and join its [4] _____ of members. Some teachers [5] _____ about the service and have stopped their students using it during school hours. They think students are [6] _____ study time. But, more importantly, the site is [7] _____ dangerous because students can share personal details. "Students might think this [8] _____ is just fun, but things can go wrong if they give information to the wrong person," a worried teacher says with [9] _____ . She wants the site to have more warnings about the risks.

| | 9 |

2 Choose the correct answers

(Circle) the correct answer: a, b or c.

1 I _____ have long hair.
   a would   b (used to)   c was used to

2 He smiled at me in a _____ way.
   a friendly   b friends   c friendliness

3 Rachel sang _____ enthusiasm, and she sounded great.
   a of   b in   c with

4 I _____ have a dog when I was a child, but I don't have any pets now.
   a would   b should   c used to

5 I answered all the questions, but _____ .
   a difficult way   b with difficulty   c with difficult

6 We _____ love that TV series.
   a used to   b use to   c use

7 The craze caught _____ immediately.
   a up   b in   c on

8 The fashion _____ swept through schools in the U.S.
   a quick   b in a quickly way   c quickly

9 Fans reacted _____ when they discovered that the tickets were sold out.
   a angrily   b with angrily   c angry

| | 8 |

3 Vocabulary

Complete each sentence with one word.

1 I had an accident because I was ___*in*___ a hurry.

2 It was a total surprise. He'd done everything _____ secret.

3 I didn't think he would want to come, but he accepted _____ great enthusiasm.

4 I deleted some files on my computer _____ accident. I was so angry with myself!

5 Can I talk to you _____ private for a few minutes?

6 Monday, Tuesday and now Wednesday – you've been late three days in a _____ .

7 I put my shorts on inside _____ .

8 The CD-ROM didn't play because I'd put it in the computer _____ down.

9 I don't think it was an accident. I'm sure he did it on _____ !

| | 8 |

How did you do?

Total: | 25 |

| 😊 | Very good 25 – 20 | 😐 | OK 19 – 16 | 😞 | Review Unit 6 again 15 or less |

7) Do something!

1 Grammar

✱ Conditionals review

a Match the two parts of the sentences. Write the letters a–h in the boxes.

1 If you want to get involved with a charity,   *d*

2 If you wanted to be useful in some way, ...

3 If she walks too fast at this altitude, ...

4 If she'd walked any faster at this altitude, ...

5 If we get lots of sponsors, ...

6 If we had more sponsors, ...

7 If he's feeling sick, ...

8 If he'd been feeling sick, ...

a she'll get a really bad headache.

b we'll raise a lot of money for the charity.

c he wouldn't have played.

d there are a lot of things you can do.

e he won't play.

f she'd have gotten a really bad headache.

g there'd be a lot of things you could do.

h we'd raise a lot of money for the charity.

b Match the sentences with the pictures. Write 1–6 in the boxes.

1 It won't be difficult if you get in shape.

2 If they'd played better, they'd have won.

3 You'd enjoy yourself more if you danced.

4 If you were in shape, it wouldn't be difficult.

5 If they play better than last week, they'll win.

6 You'd have enjoyed yourself more if you'd danced.

c Complete the sentences with the correct form of the verbs in parentheses.

1 If we'd found more sponsors, we *would have raised* (raise) more money for the charity.

2 I'd be a volunteer if I .... (have) more time.

3 If Jackie .... (go) on the charity walk next week, I'll go with her.

4 If I could go anywhere in the world, I .... (visit) the Himalayas.

5 I think I'd freeze to death if I .... (not have) my sleeping bag in the tent.

6 If I .... (not go) on the Antarctica trip, I'll regret it for the rest of my life.

7 If anyone makes a rude comment during tomorrow's game, we .... (throw) them out of the stadium.

8 We'd have won the game if the coach .... (make) us train harder.

2 Vocabulary

✳ Ways of getting involved

a Complete the puzzle.

1 We're trying to raise _____ for sick children.
2 Our charity needs money, so please make a _____ .
3 I don't get paid for this. It's _____ work.
4 We went to the mall to hand out _____ .
5 We're going to have a _____ against the new law.
6 Charities need a lot of people to _____ them out.
7 Don't just sit around and do nothing – get _____ !
8 We need lots of people to sign our _____ .
9 Eddie Izzard ran 43 _____ .

b Complete the text with the correct form of the words from Exercise 2a.

At our school, there's a big mixture of kids from different cultures, so for our charity work this year we decided to _____*raise*_____ money for "Show Racism the Red Card." It's an organization that works against racism in soccer. We decided to ¹ _____ out by organizing a soccer game between two teams, both of which had a mixture of players from different cultures on them, and we raised almost $1,500. Some other kids gave up their free time to do ² _____ work like going to the mall to hand out ³ _____ . These explained why racism is a bad thing, and asked people to make ⁴ _____ to the organization. Then the next weekend, a lot of us went to a soccer game and we ⁵ _____ outside the stadium before the game started. We also got a lot of people to sign our ⁶ _____ against racism. We got over 500 signatures! So it was a great experience, and we all learned that it's great to get ⁷ _____ in this kind of thing.

c (Vocabulary bank) Complete the sentences with words in the box.

> backed   collaborated   hand   aid
> volunteered   with   ~~worker~~

1 My brother's going to be an aid _____*worker*_____ in Central America.
2 Everyone at school _____ me when I entered the charity run.
3 If you have any problems, call me and I'll come and give you a _____ .
4 After the earthquake, hundreds of people _____ to help find survivors.
5 John and I _____ on this project – see, both our names are there.
6 They're collecting money in _____ of cancer research.
7 I only managed to do this _____ the aid of my family and friends.

3 Pronunciation

✳ Contractions in third conditionals

▶ CD4 T15 Listen and repeat. How do you pronounce the underlined sounds?

1 If you'd eaten that, you'<u>d have been</u> sick.
2 If you'd asked me, I'<u>d have</u> told you.
3 If you hadn't told him, he wouldn't <u>have</u> known!
4 I'<u>d have been</u> delighted if you'd come.
5 It would <u>have been</u> difficult if he'd been there.
6 Would you <u>have</u> come if we'd invited you?

④ Grammar
✱ Mixed conditionals

a Read the sentences. If a sentence refers to the *past only*, write PO at the end. If a sentence refers to the *past and present*, write PP at the end.

1 If we'd stayed in a different hotel, our vacation would've been better. *PO*

2 I wouldn't have had such a good time if you hadn't come with me. ....

3 If I hadn't played in the game yesterday, I wouldn't be so tired today. ....

4 I'd have taken more photos if I'd had more time. ....

5 I'd be happier if the exam had been a little easier. ....

6 I'd have gone on the charity walk if I wasn't so busy. ....

b Match the pictures with the sentences. Write 1–6 in the boxes. There are three sentences you won't need.

Ⓐ  □

Ⓑ  □

Ⓒ  □

1 If I hadn't gone on vacation, I'd be able to buy a motorcycle.

2 If I'd gone on vacation, I wouldn't be able to buy a motorcycle.

3 If I had a good memory, I'd have passed.

4 If I didn't have a good memory, I wouldn't have passed.

5 If I didn't speak Japanese, I wouldn't have understood.

6 If I spoke Japanese, I would have understood.

c Match the two parts of the sentences.

1 If I knew how to cook, *c*

2 If I had learned how to cook, ...

3 If he were a better student, ...

4 If he had been a better student in high school, ...

5 The party would be better ....

6 The party wouldn't be as good ....

7 If you saw that movie, ...

8 If you had seen that movie, ...

a if we hadn't run out of food early.

b you wouldn't have liked it.

c I would have made dinner last night.

d he would have passed the test last week.

e I could work at this restaurant.

f if we had run out of food.

g you could tell me how it ends.

h he'd be going to a better college now.

d Join the two sentences with a mixed conditional.

1 She doesn't speak Spanish. She didn't understand.
If she spoke Spanish, she would have understood.

2 I don't swim well. I didn't win the race.

....

....

3 She has worked extremely hard. She's successful.

....

....

4 My brother loves U2. He spent $200 on a ticket for their concert.

....

....

5 I hate action movies. I didn't go to see *Iron Man 2*.

....

....

Culture in mind

a Read the text and label the pictures with the correct "a-thon."

1 _____a bowl-a-thon_____

2 _____

3 _____

4 _____

5 _____

All About "A-thons"

Marathons are a popular running event. They are not only competitions, but some people have marathons for charity. Runners get friends and family to sponsor them. People pledge a certain amount of money for every kilometer. For example, if someone pledges $1, and the runner runs 10 kilometers, the person gives the runner $10 for the charity. The runners collect money from every sponsor. A lot of money can be raised for charity this way. However, not everyone can run, so people have thought of other ways to raise money, using the idea of a marathon.

Walk-a-thons

People all over the United States have walk-a-thons for all kinds of different charities. A walk-a-thon is similar to a marathon, but people walk instead of run. This is one of the most popular ways to raise money.

Dance-a-thons

In dance-a-thons, people dance to raise money for charity. Sponsors usually pledge a certain amount of money for every hour someone dances. These events are very popular with teenagers in the U.S.

Rock-a-thons

People rock in rocking chairs in rock-a-thons. Money is usually pledged for every hour someone rocks. These events are usually held in large, open places and are popular throughout the U.S. People of all ages bring their rocking chairs and rock for as long as they can!

Read-a-thons

Many U.S. schools have read-a-thons for fundraisers. Students get pledges for the number of books they read in a given amount of time. For example, they may have a month or two to read. Younger children may get pledges based on the number of pages they read. These events not only raise money, they also encourage children to read.

Bowl-a-thons

Bowling is a popular sport in the United States. In a bowl-a-thon, people bowl to raise money. They get pledges for every point they get in a game. The higher the score, the more money they make for the charity!

b Read the text again and answer the questions.

1 Why do the names of the fundraisers end in a-thon?

2 Which event gets pledges based on points?

3 Which event is the most popular fundraiser?

4 How old are the participants in rock-a-thons?

5 Which event is popular with teenagers?

6 What is a benefit to read-a-thons besides raising money?

Skills in mind

6 Read

a Greenpeace is an international environmental organization. Complete their webpage with the phrases in the box.

> let your imagination run wild   informs or inspires you
> who want to get involved   saved ancient forests from logging
> speak with one voice   will make all the difference

◄ ► C ⌂ [   ]   — E

GREENPEACE International

Make a donation

We don't accept donations from governments or corporations, so the money we need to do our work comes from people like you. Your donation
1 _____ .

Become a Cyberactivist

Our global community of Greenpeace people comes from 125 countries. We have a long list of successes to prove that when people
2 _____ ,
they can change the world. Sign up and you'll get our e-zine, a monthly electronic magazine, which is full of ways you can help. It's all free.

Visit our Action Forum

Take part in the online community that has changed climate-damaging policies, stopped the killing of hundreds of whales in Iceland,
3 _____ ,
and had many other successes. You'll get a free homepage and a chance to meet other people
4 _____ .

Spread the word!

Any time you see something on the Greenpeace site that interests,
5 _____ ,
send it to a friend. Write letters to the editor of your local paper. Buy a Greenpeace T-shirt and wear it!

GET INVOLVED

Green computer users

Are you into computers? You can help us spread the word by creating something for us. A screensaver, perhaps? A game about the environment?
6 _____

Send us your ideas using our contact form, and if it's cool and it works, we'll use it and send you a gift to say thank you.

b Read the text again. Mark each sentence *T* (true) or *F* (false).

1 Greenpeace gets money from governments. [F]

2 If you join Greenpeace, you'll get a free electronic magazine every week. [ ]

3 Greenpeace has prevented whales in Iceland from being killed. [ ]

4 Greenpeace suggests that you write letters to the editor of their newspaper. [ ]

5 Greenpeace wants people to send all kinds of information technology ideas. [ ]

6 Greenpeace will pay you if they use your ideas. [ ]

EXAM TIP

True / false exercises

- Read the statements carefully, so that you know what each one really means.

- Find the relevant part of the text for each statement.

- Watch out for expressions which are similar in meaning, for example *get money* and *receive donations*.

- There will be a mixture of true and false statements.

Unit check

1 Fill in the blanks

Complete the text with the words in the box.

| ~~raise~~ volunteers sponsored I finished I'd finished handed support involved I'd be donation |

A few weeks ago, I read about a 20 km run to _____raise_____ money for a little girl who needs an operation,
so I decided to get [1] _____ . At first, I thought about making a [2] _____ , but then I read
that they wanted [3] _____ to join the run. I thought, "If I needed an operation, [4] _____
really happy if people tried to help me." So I decided to join the run. A lot of people [5] _____ me.
If [6] _____ the run, I'd make $200 for the charity. On the day of the run, my family and friends
came to [7] _____ me. The organizers [8] _____ out numbers to all the runners. After
about 12 km, I had to stop so I didn't get all of the money from the sponsors. If [9] _____ the run,
I would have made more. I sent a check for $200 anyway.

| 9 |

2 Choose the correct answers

(Circle) the correct answer: a, b or c.

1 We're trying to _____ $1,000 for charity.
  a (raise) b rise c rest

2 Would you like to _____ a donation?
  a do b make c pay

3 We're going into town to _____ out leaflets.
  a hand b look c take

4 On Saturday, I'm going to a big _____ .
  a petition b aid c demonstration

5 We need people to _____ our work.
  a support b involve c sign

6 If you'd worn a coat, you _____ cold now.
  a wouldn't be b hadn't been c weren't

7 The charity has paid employees, but it also
needs _____ to help out.
  a frees b involvers c volunteers

8 I'd have less trouble with these questions if they
_____ easier.
  a will be b would be c were

9 If I were a better climber, I _____ to the top.
  a had gone b would have gone c went

| 8 |

3 Vocabulary

<u>Underline</u> the correct words.

1 Would you like to make a *donation / money / support* to our charity?

2 We're collecting money in *help / aid / save* of homeless people.

3 Our job will be a lot easier if we *support / demonstrate / collaborate* with each other.

4 This is really heavy. Can you give me a *help / hand / aid*?

5 I did a charity run, and I *raised / won / handed out* more than $150 for charity.

6 Nobody forced him to help with the bake sale. He's a *supporter / volunteer / donation*.

7 It's their problem, not mine. I don't want to get *volunteer / organized / involved*.

8 There's going to be a big *demonstration / marathon / petition* against racism in Boston next weekend.

9 Would you like to *hand out / sign / join* this petition?

| 8 |

How did you do?

Total: | 25 |

| ☺ | Very good 25 – 20 | ☻ | OK 19 – 16 | ☹ | Review Unit 7 again 15 or less |

8 Our world

1 Grammar

✴ Future continuous

a Here is Sara's calendar for tomorrow. Write a sentence about what she will be doing at each of the times.

1 At 8:30 a.m. tomorrow *she'll be flying to Toronto.*

2 At 10:45 a.m. tomorrow _____ .

3 At 1:00 p.m. _____ .

4 At 4:00 p.m. _____ .

5 At 5:30 p.m. _____ .

6 At 7:00 p.m. _____ .

7 At 9:45 p.m. _____ .

8 At midnight _____ .

b Write sentences about the year 2030.

1 People / live / houses under the ocean
   People will be living in houses under the ocean.

2 We / not eat / any natural food
   _____
   _____

3 Children / study / at home on computers
   _____
   _____

4 We / drive / electric cars
   _____
   _____

5 We / not use / telephones
   _____
   _____

6 People / not work / more than 25 hours a week
   _____
   _____

August 15	
8:00 – 9:10 a.m.	Fly to Toronto
10:30 – 11:30 a.m.	Discuss the new Toronto store with George
12:00 – 1:30 p.m.	Have lunch with Eileen Wilcox
2:00 – 5:00 p.m.	Interview people for the store manager's job
5:00 – 6:00 p.m.	Visit the company factory
6:15 – 7:30 p.m.	Look at the new designs
9:10 – 10:20 p.m.	Fly back to Detroit
11:00 p.m. – 12:30 a.m.	Watch a movie on TV!

2 Grammar

✴ Future perfect

a Complete the sentences with the future perfect forms of the verbs in brackets.

1 I __*will have finished*__ (finish) my homework by 10:00.

2 I think they _____ (find) a cure for cancer by 2025.

3 By 2090, the world's population _____ (increase) to about 30 billion.

4 Please don't call me at 3:00. I _____ (not leave) school by then.

5 Next year, my parents _____ (be) married for 25 years.

6 How _____ (our lives / change) by the year 2050?

7 Go and buy a ticket before noon, otherwise they _____ (sell) them all.

Today

20 years later

b Use the words to write sentences about the future of the town in the pictures.

1 They / build / airport
   They will have built an airport.

2 The school / disappear

   _____

3 The river / dry up

   _____

4 The stores / become / supermarket

   _____

5 They / close down / factory

   _____

6 They / put / parking lot underground

   _____

7 People / put / solar panels / the roofs of their houses

   _____

c (Circle) the correct tense, future continuous or future perfect.

1 Don't call me at 8:00 tonight because we'll (be having) / have had dinner then.

2 When I'm 25, we'll _be living_ / _have lived_ in the U.S. for five years.

3 At 11:00 tomorrow morning, I _will have taken_ / _will be taking_ a test.

4 By the end of the weekend, my brother _will have played_ / _will be playing_ five soccer games!

5 If you want to see the game, come over this afternoon, when we _will be watching_ / _will have watched_ it.

6 Next Wednesday morning, we _will be sitting_ / _will have sat_ on the beach in Mexico!

3 Pronunciation

✱ /ð/ _the_ and /θ/ _thing_

a ▶ CD4 T16 Listen and put the words in the correct place.

> other   bathtub   month   brother
> theater   clothes   ~~thin~~   weather
> Thursday   this

/θ/ _thing_	/ð/ _the_
thin	

b ▶ CD4 T17 Listen and repeat.

1 I think their brother is thin.

2 There are three rooms with a bathtub.

3 I thought I saw them at the theater last month.

4 My mother went there on Thursday.

4 Vocabulary

✱ Global issues

a Complete the text with the words in the box.

> waste   starvation   species
> temperature   ~~resources~~   atmosphere

Making the future **brighter** ?

Many of the world's natural _____resources_____ are running out, and the [1] _____ of the sea is going up, increasing the chances of polar ice melting. Global warming is also increasing due to pollution in the [2] _____ , mainly because of the use of fossil fuels like coal and oil. We could use more nuclear energy, but what do we do with the [3] _____ ? And then there is the fact that many [4] _____ of animal are becoming extinct, and members of our own human race are dying through [5] _____ and war. What can we do? Well, let's look at some ideas…

b Replace the words in *italics* with the correct form of the verbs in the box.

bring about   die out   use up   get rid of   make up for   go up

❶ Support organizations that are trying to ~~cause~~ *bring about* an end to trade in rare animals.

❷ Don't buy medicines and other products that result in animals *becoming extinct* _____ .

❸ Remember that every time you travel by car or plane, you cause the temperature of the air to *increase* _____ .

❹ Don't try to *compensate for* _____ using too much water by donating money to the poor.

❺ You don't need all those electrical machines. *Dispose of* _____ some of them!

❻ Remember that if we go on using oil and coal the way we do, they will be *completely finished* _____ in a few years.

❺ Study help

✴ Learning phrasal verbs

● **The meanings of phrasal verbs**
You should make a note of new phrasal verbs in a vocabulary notebook, including the new item in a sentence which clearly shows its meaning.

My sister and I made up five minutes after we argued.

Other methods you can use include synonyms. However, you must remember that these words will not always be directly interchangeable. It's also a good idea to make a note of some of the common collocations you'll find with the phrasal verb.

make up with someone

You should also note any other meanings. *Make up can also mean to invent a story, e.g., My father made up a lot of stories to tell me when I was little.*

Check the register (degree of formality). Phrasal verbs are often (but not always) colloquial and more commonly used in spoken language.

Finally, you might translate the words into your first language.

● **Grouping phrasal verbs**
Some students like to use grouping to help them learn sets of new phrasal verbs.

– grouping by verb (e.g., *stand by someone / stand up for something / stand in for someone*)

– grouping by preposition (e.g., *turn on / bring on / get on*)

– grouping by topic (e.g., trips – *a plane takes off / set off on an adventure / get back from vacation*)

Circle the correct phrasal verbs to complete the text.

OUR GLOBAL VILLAGE

Wherever you are these days, you will [1] (*come across*) / *meet up with* products that are available globally, even if you are a long way from home. Fast food restaurants [2] *take up / turn up* in smaller towns. City dwellers are never far from a can of Coca-Cola or Pepsi. There is always a Hollywood movie playing at a movie theater near you to [3] *sit out / sit back* and enjoy. Supporters of globalization say it gives developing countries a chance to [4] *bring back / turn into* richer, more powerful economies through tourism and trade. Why should people [5] *turn down / take back* the chance to have a better lifestyle? Others say that workers in developing countries continue to [6] *take on / put up* lower-paying jobs, even if they may now work for a global company. Can globalization help end poverty? Or does it just make the rich even richer? Whatever the answer, we should [7] *stand up for / put up with* people in poverty. We have to [8] *look into / look up* the ways that big, international companies work and try to make sure that they are as fair as possible for everyone.

6 Everyday English

a Complete the expressions with the words in the box.

~~ever~~   break   face   mind   business

1   what *ever*
2   Are you out of your _____ ?
3   Give me a _____ !
4   It's none of your _____ .
5   Let's _____ it…

b Complete the dialogue with the expressions in Exercise 6a.

Nick: Hey, Mike, do you want to go out tonight?

Mike: I can't. I have to get up tomorrow at four in the morning.

Nick: Four o'clock. [1] _____ ? Why on earth would anyone want to get up at that time?

Mike: Well, [2] _____ actually.

Nick: Oh, come on. Tell me.

Mike: OK. But I don't want any of your usual comments.

Nick: I promise I won't say anything.

Mike: We're going on an anti-global warming demonstration in Washington, D.C., and I have to catch an early bus.

Nick: Anti-global warming? [3] _____ . You don't really believe in that nonsense, do you?

Mike: You promised you wouldn't say anything.

Nick: I know, but … . Even if it's true, you're not going to change anything by going to a silly demonstration.
[4] _____ , Mike, you're just wasting your time.

Mike: [5] _____ , Nick. I'm not really that interested in what you think, and I have to get going anyway.

Nick: So who else is going to this demonstration?

Mike: Just me, Tom and his girlfriend Julia and Debbie Hanson.

Nick: Debbie Hanson? Oh. Is it too late to get a ticket?

Mike: Wait a minute! You've just been telling me what a waste of time it all is, and now you suddenly want to come along?

Nick: Well, with Debbie being there that puts it in a different light.

7 Study help

✱ Noticing language

- When you read texts in English or listen to people speaking English, you will mainly be trying to understand the message. But it can be very useful to notice not only *what* people say or write, but also *how* they say or write it.

- You probably know that there are some areas of English that you are unsure about. You might have problems with tenses (for example, the present perfect) or with words (for example, the difference between *until* and *by*).

- Make a note of any areas you feel unsure about. Then, when you are reading something, see if the text has any examples of this. If it does, stop and read again. Which words or verb tense did the person use to express their meaning? Try to remember these examples.

- You will remember these things better the more times you read or hear them. You will notice more if you read and listen to as much English as you can.

8 Write

a Read this letter quickly and answer the questions.

1 What is the person writing about?

2 What does he hope will happen?

b Read the letter again. Mark the statements *T* (true) or *F* (false).

1 The writer says he is completely against the proposal for a new supermarket. | F |

2 He thinks it's important to look at the positive and negative sides of the issue. | |

3 He does not believe that the supermarket will bring jobs for young people. | |

4 The writer will find shopping more convenient if there is a supermarket. | |

5 There are delivery trucks on the roads in the complex now. | |

6 The writer hopes that the local authorities will listen to what people think. | |

c Imagine a large change to the area where you live. This could be:

an airport
a new road
new buildings (factories / stores / supermarkets)
your own idea

Write a letter to a newspaper. Describe the planned change and its possible effects, and how you feel about them.

WRITING TIP

Rhetorical questions

- A rhetorical question is a question that we ask without really expecting an answer from anyone. It is a question asked to make an impact on the listener or reader.

- Find and <u>underline</u> three rhetorical questions that Tom asks in his letter. For each one, decide what he meant.

Readers' thoughts

Dear Sir,

There is a plan to build a new supermarket on the edge of the Sunview housing complex, on the land where the local library is now. I live in Sunview, and I would like to express my concern about this plan. It is not that I am completely against the idea of building a supermarket. I just think that as a community we need to weigh the advantages and disadvantages before committing ourselves.

It is clear that the library is underused and in poor condition. It is also clear that there are very few stores near here, and a supermarket would be a good thing to have. But the people who want to build the supermarket seem to think that no one wants the library anymore and that it isn't needed because of the Internet and so on. Is this necessarily true, especially for elderly people? What about young people who don't have Internet at home and need to go to the library to do their homework? Where can they study if they have to share a room with a younger brother or sister?

On the other hand, there is an argument that a new supermarket would not only bring more choice of shopping and more convenience for local residents, but it would also bring some much-needed jobs for younger people in the town, and this is a good point.

What we need to do is consider the effect a supermarket will have on our quality of life. Certainly the residents of the housing complex (including me) will find shopping a lot easier and more convenient. But there will also be more traffic. In a few years from now, the roads in and around the complex will be full of cars in the daytime and delivery trucks at night, and, not only that, we will have gotten used to it, too. Are more jobs and more convenience worth such an impact on our daily lives? Perhaps, but this is what we have to ask ourselves.

I believe that all the residents of Sunview, and the local authorities, need to discuss this question in an open-minded way – and I hope that by the time a decision is made, we will have had a full and fair discussion of the issues involved, and that the local authorities will have really listened to everyone's views. Is that too much to ask?

Sincerely,
Tom Watkins

Unit check

1 Fill in the blanks

Complete the text with the words in the box.

> ~~resources~~   will be   species   will have   bring about
> have become   starvation   dying   is going   will need

Animals are one of the most important __resources__ for humans, especially farm animals. But in the past 100 years, over 1,000 breeds of animal [1] _____ extinct. Still today, some [2] _____ of farm and domestic animals are [3] _____ out. This is a major problem, because the number of people in the world [4] _____ up. Some scientists say that by 2050, the population [5] _____ doubled. This means that in 40 years we [6] _____ more food to feed the world. A UN representative said, "We probably have until 2020 to stop the process. If we don't, then we [7] _____ losing some species at the rate of two a week. We have to [8] _____ a change of attitude. If we don't, this will increase the risk of [9] _____ in the future."

| 9 |

2 Choose the correct answers

Circle the correct answer: a, b or c.

1 By 2030, many species will have _____ .
  a used up   b (died out)   c gone up

2 If the world's _____ goes up any more, there won't be enough cold water in the ocean.
  a temperature   b atmosphere   c pollution

3 Don't call me after nine. I will _____ .
  a leave   b have left   c be left

4 I need to _____ some old clothes.
  a make up for   b bring about   c get rid of

5 In 100 years we'll all _____ on another planet.
  a live   b be living   c have lived

6 We have the _____ to end hunger.
  a resources   b starvation   c species

7 If we go on like this, we're going to _____ all our planet's resources. There won't be any left.
  a die out   b compensate for   c use up

8 This time next week, I will _____ on a beach in Brazil. I can't wait.
  a sit   b be sitting   c have sat

9 The game will _____ by the time we get there!
  a have finished   b be finished   c finish

| 8 |

3 Vocabulary

Underline the correct words.

1 The black rhino is in danger of dying *up / out / over* in the next few years.
2 Why didn't you tell me you've used *out / under / up* all the printer ink?
3 Don't you think it's time you got rid *of / out / about* that teddy bear? You're 15!
4 I was wrong but I want to make *out / above / up* for it.
5 Buy the TV now. It's going *over / above / up* by $200 at the end of the week.
6 We need a president who will bring *about / up / around* real change.
7 There are more than 10,000 *species / resources / makes* of birds in the world.
8 There's no reason why anyone in the modern world should die of *waste / temperature / starvation*.
9 They don't have the *waste / atmosphere / resources* to deal with such a huge natural disaster.

| 8 |

How did you do?

Total: | 25 |

| 😊 | Very good 25 – 20 | 😐 | OK 19 – 16 | ☹ | Review Unit 8 again 15 or less |

9 Peacemakers

1 Grammar

★ Past perfect passive

a (Circle) the past perfect passive to complete the sentences.

1 I couldn't believe it! I *was /* (*had been*) chosen to play on the baseball team.

2 I *was / had been* told to get off the bus at the last stop.

3 The lottery winnings *were / had been* shared by ten people this week.

4 When they opened the door, they saw the painting *was / had been* stolen.

5 I was so angry when I found that my diary *was / had been* read by someone.

6 Everyone in the Olympic stadium stood up and clapped. The world record *was / had been* broken.

7 When she said "no" all my dreams *were / had been* instantly destroyed.

b Tim wasn't home when his parents returned early from their vacation. Look at the picture and use the words to make sentences.

1 vase / break

   A vase had been broken.

2 front window / leave open

   ....

3 sofa / tear

   ....

4 TV / leave on

   ....

5 books and CDs / not put away

   ....

c Rewrite the sentences using the past perfect passive. Use the word in **bold** at the end.

1 When we got to the party, there wasn't any food left. (**eaten**)

   When we got to the party, all the food had been eaten.

2 I opened my bag and saw that my wallet wasn't there. (**stolen**)

   ....

3 The street was very different because there were no more trees there. (**cut down**)

   ....

4 When I got home, the TV was working again. (**fixed**)

   ....

5 I didn't go to the party because no one sent me an invitation. (**invited**)

   ....

6 We didn't watch the TV show because we didn't know about it. (**told**)

   ....

Grammar

★ Past perfect continuous

a In 2004, Wangari Maathai received the Nobel Peace Prize for her environmental work in Kenya. Read the text about her and her Green Belt Movement and complete the text with the words in the box.

> been causing   not studied
> become known   been developing   spent
> played   ~~always been~~   been fighting

Kenyan president Daniel Arap Moi and his government had _always been_ happy to help out big business even if this wasn't always best for the environment. At the same time, Wangari Maathai and her Green Belt Movement had ¹_____ to save the land.

Ever since the organization started in 1977, it had ²_____ the Kenyan government problems. In 1989, the two sides met for their biggest showdown.

That year, the Green Belt Movement learned that powerful friends of the president had ³_____ plans to build a 60-floor office building in the heart of Uhuru Park in the capital city Nairobi. The park had ⁴_____ an important part in city life for many years, and it was the only place in Nairobi where families could go and enjoy the outdoors. When the Movement launched its campaign against the "monster-park" as the building had ⁵_____ , Wangari Maathai was often laughed at in public for not understanding development. Although she was the first to admit that she had ⁶_____ town planning in college, she was smart enough to know that you need such spaces in large cities. Luckily, so were thousands of other Kenyans who joined the campaign and the park was saved. But the victory didn't finish there. The very same government who had ⁷_____ so much time laughing at Maathai and her movement have now made Uhuru Park a national park.

b Use the verb in **bold** and the past perfect (once) or the past perfect continuous (once) to complete each pair of sentences.

1 **(walk)**
   a We were hungry because we _had been walking_ all day.
   b When we got back to the hotel we _had walked_ 20 km.

2 **(read)**
   a By the end of the summer vacation, I _____ the three *Lord of the Rings* books.
   b I _____ for two hours, so when I turned out the light, I fell asleep immediately.

3 **(save)**
   a I started in March, and by October I _____ enough money for my trip to South Korea.
   b I _____ for two years, but I still didn't have enough money.

4 **(eat)**
   a We _____ all day and I couldn't eat any more.
   b When he arrived, we _____ everything, so I made him a quick sandwich.

5 **(watch)**
   a He got a headache because he _____ TV all day.
   b By the end of the evening, we _____ all six *Star Wars* movies.

6 **(talk)**
   a When I saw her yesterday she _____ to her teacher, and she was feeling better.
   b She _____ on the phone for so long that she was really thirsty.

7 **(cook)**
   a He _____ all morning, and there was a great smell coming from the kitchen.
   b He _____ me a birthday meal. I was so happy.

8 **(write)**
   a My hand was aching because I _____ since 10 o'clock.
   b I _____ the letter, but was I brave enough to send it?

3 Vocabulary

✱ Conflicts and solutions

a Read the newspaper article and circle the correct answer: a, b, c or d.

Did you have a falling ¹ _out_ with an old friend? Do you need to sort things ² _____ with a member of your family? Or do you want to make ³ _____ with your boyfriend or girlfriend?

If your answer to any of these questions is "yes," then don't worry – help is here. *The Record* is proud to welcome one of the country's top advice columnists, Claire Jones, who will be writing exclusively for our paper as of next week. Claire has more than 20 years' experience of helping people ⁴ _____ compromises and ⁵ _____ conflicts. Claire knows that there are always two people to listen to and promises not to take ⁶ _____ .

By ⁷ _____ neutral, Claire is confident she can give you the advice you need to get your life back on track. So if you have a problem and are ⁸ _____ , drop Claire a line today.

askclaire@therecord.cup

1 a up b in c (out) d on
2 a out b over c with d for
3 a in b up c on d down
4 a get b have c look d reach
5 a resolve b finish c break d fix
6 a issues b part c sides
   d perspective
7 a waiting b staying c having
   d finding
8 a stuck b broken c missing
   d fixed

b [Vocabulary bank] Complete the dialogue with the words in the box.

> ~~quarrel~~ pick a fight give-and-take to the bottom
> on speaking terms misunderstanding negotiate
> ill feeling by the horns come to blows

Ana: Did I detect a bit of ¹ _____ between you and Dan today?

Matt: Yes. We're not ² _____ .

Ana: Again! So what did you ³ _quarrel_ about this time?

Matt: I'm not sure really. I think he just wanted to ⁴ _____ with someone, and I happened to be in the wrong place at the wrong time.

Ana: What? He hit you?

Matt: No, no. It didn't ⁵ _____ . He just started shouting at me for some reason.

Ana: There must have been a reason. Don't you want to get ⁶ _____ of it?

Matt: Well, there was a ⁷ _____ about his bike, but I'm not sure exactly what I did.

Ana: Do you want me to say something to him for you?

Matt: What? Try and ⁸ _____ with Dan? You'll be wasting your time.

Ana: I don't understand you and Dan – best friends but always having a falling out. You know it's all about ⁹ _____ , don't you?

Matt: You should take the bull ¹⁰ _____ and tell that to Dan. Then maybe he wouldn't get so angry when I take his bike without asking.

4 Pronunciation

✱ Linking sounds

a ▶ CD4 T18 Listen and look at the underlined sounds. Check (✓) the sentence in each pair where the hard consonant sound disappears.

1 a Have they ma<u>de</u> up yet? ☐
   b She ma<u>de</u> Paul apologize. ☐

2 a Let's try and <u>sort</u> out the problem. ☐
   b Let's try and <u>sort</u> the problem out. ☐

3 a Why do you always <u>take</u> sides? ☐
   b Can you <u>take</u> out the trash? ☐

4 a I always <u>get</u> stuck when I do math. ☐
   b <u>Get</u> out of my room. I'm working. ☐

b ▶ CD4 T18 Listen and repeat.

5 Fiction in mind

Read the extract from *Lord of the Flies* by William Golding. Ralph, who was the leader, is being chased by some of the boys.

He stumbled over a root and the cry that [1]<u>pursued</u> him rose even higher. [...] Then he was down, rolling over and over in the warm sand, crouching with arm up to ward off, trying to cry for mercy.

He staggered to his feet, tensed for more terrors, and looked up at a huge peaked cap. [...]

A naval officer stood on the sand, looking down at Ralph in wary astonishment. On the beach behind him was a [2]<u>cutter</u>, her bows hauled up and held by two ratings. In the stern-sheets another rating held a sub-machine gun. [...]

The officer looked at Ralph doubtfully for a moment, then took his hand away from the butt of the revolver.

"Hullo."

Squirming a little, conscious of his filthy appearance, Ralph answered shyly.

"Hullo."

The officer nodded, as if a question had been answered.

"Are there any adults – any grown-ups with you?"

[3]<u>Dumbly</u>, Ralph shook his head. He turned a half-pace on the sand. A semicircle of little boys, their bodies streaked with colored clay, sharp sticks in their hands, were standing on the beach making no noise at all.

"Fun and games," said the officer. [...]

The officer [4]<u>grinned</u> cheerfully at Ralph.

"We saw your smoke. What have you been doing? Having a war or something?"

Ralph nodded.

The officer inspected the little scarecrow in front of him. The kid needed a bath, a hair-cut, a nose-wipe and a good deal of ointment.

"Nobody killed, I hope? Any dead bodies?"

"Only two. And they're gone."

The officer leaned down and looked closely at Ralph.

"Two? Killed?"

Ralph nodded again. Behind him, the whole island was shuddering with flames. The officer knew, [5]<u>as a rule</u>, when people were telling the truth. He whistled softly. [...]

"We'll take you off. How many of you are there?"

Ralph shook his head. The officer looked past him to the group of painted boys.

"Who's boss here?"

"I am," said Ralph loudly.

A little boy who wore the remains of an extraordinary black cap on his red hair and who carried the remains of a pair of spectacles at his waist, stepped forward, then changed his mind and stood still.

"We saw your smoke. And you don't know how many of you there are?"

"No, sir."

"I should have thought," said the officer as he visualized the search before him, "I should have thought that a [6]<u>pack</u> of British boys – you're all British, aren't you? – would have been able to put up a better show than that – I mean – "

"It was like that at first,' said Ralph, "before things – "

He stopped.

"We were together, then – "

The officer nodded helpfully.

---

a (Circle) the word or phrase that is closest in meaning to the <u>underlined</u> words in the text.

1 a followed   b covered   c hurt

2 a pair of scissors   b small boat   c sailor

3 a Smiling   b Without speaking   c Laughing

4 a smiled   b shouted   c waved

5 a for sure   b as an officer   c usually

6 a group   b school   c number

b Read the text again and answer the questions.

1 The officer takes his hand away from his revolver. Why do you think his hand was on the revolver?

2 When Ralph says, "Hullo," he answers an unspoken question. What do you think is the question?

3 The officer says, "Fun and games" and then he smiles. What does he think is happening?

4 Does the officer believe it when Ralph says two boys were killed? How do you know?

5 Ralph says "before things –" but he doesn't finish the sentence. What do you think he was going to say?

6 Write

Bank Plc Ltd   20 87 122

SAMARITAN OF
THE YEAR

$1,000.00

103 87 401 41441 0111

Wanted – Samaritan of the Year

Do you have a colleague at work or school who is always ready to help out anyone in need? Is your next-door neighbor a tireless campaigner for charity? Do you know anyone who'd never say "I'm sorry, I'm too busy"?

If your answer to any of these questions was "yes," then you might just be the person to help us find our Samaritan of the Year.

Send us an email (no longer than 300 words), telling us who this person is and exactly why they deserve the title, and you could find yourself on the front page of our paper with your Samaritan.

And there's more. As well as instant fame, your Samaritan will win $1,000 to donate to a charity of his or her choice – so don't forget to tell us what this charity is and why your Samaritan has chosen it.

a What do you think a Samaritan is? Check (✓) the best definition 1, 2 or 3. Read the advertisement to check.

1 someone who works for charity ☐

2 someone who helps other people ☐

3 a good friend ☐

b Read the advertisement again and <u>underline</u> four pieces of information that should be included in every competition entry.

c A student has written a reply to the advertisement. Read the email and answer the questions.

1 Who is Paul Scott?

2 Why is he being nominated?

3 What charity will the money go to and why?

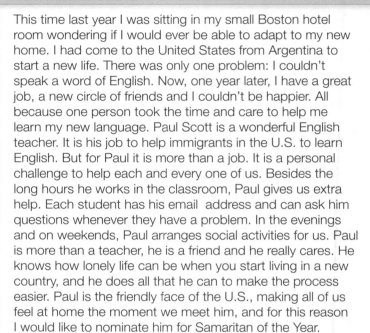

This time last year I was sitting in my small Boston hotel room wondering if I would ever be able to adapt to my new home. I had come to the United States from Argentina to start a new life. There was only one problem: I couldn't speak a word of English. Now, one year later, I have a great job, a new circle of friends and I couldn't be happier. All because one person took the time and care to help me learn my new language. Paul Scott is a wonderful English teacher. It is his job to help immigrants in the U.S. to learn English. But for Paul it is more than a job. It is a personal challenge to help each and every one of us. Besides the long hours he works in the classroom, Paul gives us extra help. Each student has his email address and can ask him questions whenever they have a problem. In the evenings and on weekends, Paul arranges social activities for us. Paul is more than a teacher, he is a friend and he really cares. He knows how lonely life can be when you start living in a new country, and he does all that he can to make the process easier. Paul is the friendly face of the U.S., making all of us feel at home the moment we meet him, and for this reason I would like to nominate him for Samaritan of the Year.

If Paul wins, he will donate the money to New Home, a charity that works to help immigrants adapt to their new life, because it is a charity that has helped many people and Paul would like to support them.

d Write your entry for the competition.

WRITING TIP

Writing an entry for a competition

- As always, read through the instructions carefully and underline or highlight the key points. Make sure you answer all of these.

- It is good to use the key points to help you organize your writing. How and in what order are you going to answer them?

- Can you think of a way of making your entry stand out from the rest? Perhaps you could start with a funny story or a quotation. Or you could use anecdotes – little stories about your experiences. This will make your writing more personal and interesting to the reader.

1 Fill in the blanks

Complete the text with the words in the box.

with	traveling	about	had	for
~~was~~	been	arrived	what	from

The very first Nobel Peace Prize ___was___ awarded to Jean Henri Dunant, a Swiss businessman [1] _____
Geneva. In 1859, Dunant's travels took him to the small town of Solferino, which today is in Italy. He had
been [2] _____ all day when he [3] _____ and found that the town had [4] _____ the scene
of a battle between Napoleon's French army and the Austrian army. More than 30,000 men [5] _____
been killed or seriously wounded. Dunant was shocked by [6] _____ he saw, and he decided to stay
and help [7] _____ the injured. He wrote [8] _____ his experiences in a book called *A Memory
of Solferino*. This book became the inspiration [9] _____ the creation of the International Red Cross,
whose mission is to protect human life and health.

| | 9 |

2 Choose the correct answers

Circle the correct answer: a, b or c.

1 Do you know if Steve and Janice have made _____
   yet or are they still not speaking?
   a to   b on   c **up**

2 All the seats had _____ taken so we had to stand.
   a be   b been   c being

3 Why do you always _____ his side in every argument?
   a go on   b make   c take

4 When we arrived we were exhausted because we
   _____ for almost 15 hours.
   a had flown   b had flying   c had been flying

5 I've had a falling _____ with my friend because she
   didn't invite me to her party this weekend.
   a out   b on   c in

6 We were late, and when we arrived at the party, they
   _____ "Happy Birthday" already.
   a had sung   b have been singing   c had been singing

7 I got _____ on this problem and need some help.
   a caught   b stuck   c frozen

8 I think we need to _____ a few things before we go
   any further.
   a sort out   b compromise   c mend

9 Their wedding cake _____ made by his mother. It was
   beautiful.
   a had   b has been   c had been

| | 8 |

3 Vocabulary

**Replace the underlined words with a
phrase using the word in parentheses.**

1 I try not to take sides when mom and
   dad quarrel. **(neutral)** ___stay neutral___

2 Bob and Amy aren't speaking to each
   other. **(falling)** _____

3 It was a serious argument and they
   almost started fighting. **(blows)**
   _____

4 I think they're friends again. **(made)**
   _____

5 They've found a solution which is
   OK for both of them. **(compromise)**
   _____

6 The UN is doing all it can to find a
   way to stop the fighting. **(resolve)**
   _____

7 My sisters refuse to talk to each other.
   (terms) _____

8 Tim always looks for things to argue
   about. **(pick)** _____

9 You and your dad need to find a way
   of resolving your problems. **(sort)**
   _____

| | 8 |

How did you do?

Total: | 25 |

☺	Very good 25 – 20	
☺	OK 19 – 16	
☹	Review Unit 9 again 15 or less	

1 Grammar

★ *It* as subject with infinitives

a Put the words in the correct order to make sentences.

1 to / it / lonely / feel / hurts
  It hurts to feel lonely.

2 wonderful / it's / kind / be / to
  ....

3 it / good / people / to / see / smile / feels
  ....

4 to / you're / it's / say / sorry / important
  ....

5 isn't / be / hard / it / nice / to / people / other / to
  ....

6 help / it / anything / cost / to / doesn't / people
  ....

7 stressed / not / unusual / to / who / are / see / people / it's
  ....

8 difficult / it's / don't / to / why / each / other / people / talk / to / understand
  ....

c Rewrite the sentences to start with *It*.

1 Skateboarding in traffic? That's crazy!
  It's crazy to skateboard in traffic.

2 Having a good time in this town is hard.
  ....

3 Making new friends is fun.
  ....

4 Helping other people is nice.
  ....

5 Smiling doesn't hurt.
  ....

6 You forget people's names sometimes. That's normal.
  ....

7 Being kind to other people doesn't cost anything.
  ....

8 Seeing other people smile when you help them is wonderful.
  ....

b Match the sentences with the people in the pictures. Write 1–6 in the boxes.

A

B

C

D [1]

E

F

1 It's difficult to see where we're going.
2 It's important to exchange our details.
3 It isn't easy to live in the city.
4 It's difficult to know which one to get.
5 It's fun to try new things.
6 It's great to see you again!

2 Vocabulary

✱ Making an effort

a Complete the puzzle using the clues 1–7.

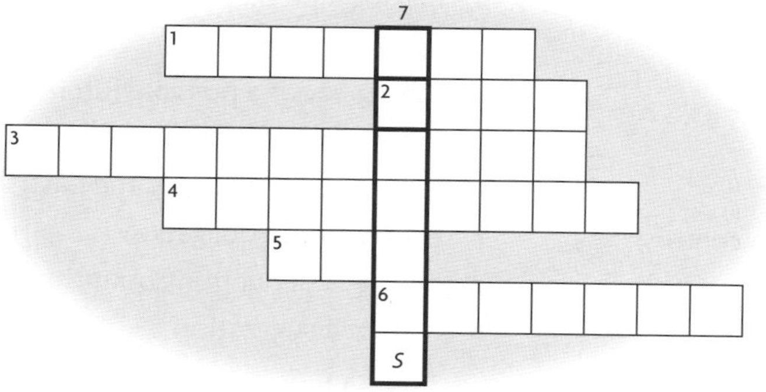

(crossword grid with numbered cells 1–7, including an "s" in the shaded vertical column)

1 We saw an interesting trail, so we decided to go hiking on an _____ .

2 I don't always find it _____ to solve problems.

3 My friend's father offered me a job, so I decided to seize the _____ .

4 The instructions were really complicated, and I _____ for hours to understand them.

5 I loved the theater workshops, and I think I got a lot _____ of them.

6 I wasn't really into playing the game, so I only made a half-_____ attempt.

7 My parents went to great _____ to pay for me to go to college.

b Complete the text with the expressions in the box. There is one expression you won't use.

struggled	~~find it easy~~	got a lot out of it
seize the opportunity	half-hearted	
go to great lengths	on an impulse	

Last week there was a problem with my computer. Now, I don't _find it easy_ to work with computers, but I will ¹_____ to not spend money, so I decided to fix it myself. I ²_____ to find out what the problem was, and I finally fixed it. But I must have done something wrong because two days later, the problem was back – and worse! Although I knew I wouldn't be able to fix it, I made a ³_____ attempt for about an hour. Of course, it didn't work. I took my computer to a store, so a technician could look at it. ⁴_____ , I bought a new computer instead of getting my old one fixed! I get one year of free classes with my purchase. I'm definitely going to ⁵_____ and learn as much as I can about my new computer.

c Vocabulary bank

Complete the text with the correct form of the words in the box.

| sweat | bother | can | be |
| ~~put~~ | make | | |

My husband _put_ everything into making our anniversary a day to remember. He spent hours ¹_____ over the Internet to find us somewhere special to eat. He ²_____ a real attempt to dress up, which is something I know he hates doing. He even ³_____ to polish his shoes! And it ⁴_____ really worth the effort because he looked great. Yes, my husband really tried his hardest to make things special. It's just a shame he ⁵_____ be bothered to check the calendar and get the right day!

3 Pronunciation

✱ Linking sounds: intrusive /w/ and /y/

a Read the sentences aloud to yourself. Write *w* or *y*: *w* if the underlined sounds have a linking "w" sound; *y* if they have a linking "y" sound.

1 You and I have to talk about it. _____ *w*

2 I am going to send my sister a birthday gift. _____

3 I think I'm too old to play these games. _____

4 I wish he'd go away. _____

5 It's so easy to do. _____

6 She asked for a ride. _____

b ► CD4 T19 Listen and check. Then listen again and repeat.

4 Grammar

✱ Modal verbs review

a Match the sentences 1–8 with the explanations a–h.

1. We couldn't leave school before we were 16. ...*d*...
2. I think it'll rain tomorrow. ....
3. I must remember to call her today. ....
4. You could try being nice to people. ....
5. May I borrow your newspaper? ....
6. It must have been difficult to live in the 19th century. ....
7. I've invited him, but he might not come. ....
8. I could already play the violin when I was eight. ....

a. making a prediction
b. asking for permission
c. talking about a possible future event
d. expressing a past prohibition
e. talking about ability in the past
f. expressing an obligation
g. making a deduction about the past
h. making a suggestion

b Circle the correct answers.

1. I'm not sure yet, but I *will* / *might* go to Spain for my birthday.
2. Let's give him a book. He*'ll* / *can* like that.
3. If we don't go to her party, she*'ll* / *'d* feel awful.
4. She's a terrible dancer, so you *shouldn't* / *won't* dance with her.
5. I forgot her birthday last year, so I *must* / *can't* forget it again this year.
6. I'm sorry I forgot, but I promise I*'ll* / *should* get you a present tomorrow.
7. Thank you for the present. *Can* / *Will* I open it now?
8. Well, we haven't been invited to the party, so I think we *couldn't* / *shouldn't* go.

c Underline the correct verb to complete each dialogue.

1. "What am I going to get my dad for his birthday?"
   "Well, he likes music, so I think you *may* / <u>should</u> get him a CD."
2. "Jill's going to be 19 next week."
   "That *can't* / *shouldn't* be right because she's still in high school!"
3. "Did you like the book I gave you? I haven't read it yet."
   "Yes, it's wonderful. You really *can* / *must* read it."
4. "I'm going to the store to get stuff for the party."
   "OK. *Can* / *Would* I come with you?"
5. "I wonder how old our teacher is."
   "Well, you *won't* / *can't* ask her, she might not like it."
6. "My grandfather will be 85 next week, and he's throwing a party."
   "Great. If I were 85, I *won't* / *wouldn't* have the energy for a party!"

d Complete what each person is saying with an appropriate modal verb. There is sometimes more than one possible answer.

1. I _____ find that ring!
2. Excuse me. _____ I use your phone?
3. No, that _____ be the right way to do it!
4. I'm not sure, but I think they _____ be tourists!
5. I _____ do that if you paid me – I'm much too scared!
6. You _____ have eaten too much at the restaurant.

5 Read

a Read the text about Annie Lennox. Some lines have an extra word which should not be there. If the line is correct, write a check (✓). If a word should not be there, cross it out and write the word at the end of the line.

Annie Lennox began her recording career as the lead singer of the British	1	✓
pop band the Tourists, but after three years and only moderate success she has	2	*has*
left with band mate Dave Stewart to form the duo Eurythmics. It was	3	
with Eurythmics that Annie who began to enjoy a considerable amount of	4	
recognition, not only in the UK, but also in many countries around of the world.	5	
In the 1990s, Annie embarked on a solo career and continued where	6	
Eurythmics left off, with several bestselling albums. In 2010, she released her	7	
fifth solo album. She has won a number of music awards which including eight	8	
BRIT awards, a Golden Globe and an Oscar for "Into the West," which she	9	
wrote for the soundtrack to *The Lord of the Rings: The Return of the King.*	10	
As well as having been a hugely successful career as a musician, Annie is	11	
also a political and social activist, working tirelessly for better health awareness	12	
in Africa, and campaigning for the peace in the Middle East.	13	

b Read the text again. Mark the statements *T* (true) or *F* (false). Correct the false statements.

1 Annie Lennox has been in three bands.

   ----

2 The Tourists were a very popular band.

   ----

3 Eurythmics were popular worldwide.

   ----

4 Annie won an Oscar for her role in *The Lord of the Rings: The Return of the King.*

   ----

5 Annie is involved in issues outside of pop music.

   ----

c ▶ **CD4 T20** Listen to the biography of Al Green and answer the questions.

1 What success did Al Green have as a child?
2 What success did Al Green have in the early 1970s?
3 What two incidents had a major effect on Al Green's life?
4 How did they change his life?
5 When did he return to recording popular music?
6 What kind of records does he make these days?
7 What two people did Al Green sing duets with?
8 When did he win his ninth Grammy?
9 Which album reached number nine on the charts?

Skills in mind

6 Listen

a ▶ CD4 T21 Listen to the story and put the pictures in the correct order.

A

B

C

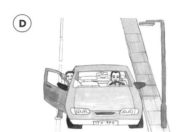
D

E

F

b ▶ CD4 T21 Listen again and answer the questions.

1 Where was the speaker going, and what was he going to do?

2 What was the title of the song he was listening to?

3 Why was the man pushing his car?

4 How old was the small boy?

5 How far did they push the car?

6 Why was the speaker so surprised at the end?

LISTENING TIP

Listening to stories

When you listen to someone telling a story or an anecdote in a casual conversation, you'll notice many important things that can help you understand better.

- The verb tense that the person uses might be past, or it might be present, or it might be a mixture of both. Which is it in this story?

- The person telling the story usually hasn't planned what to say, so sometimes he or she will start to say something, and then start again in a different way. Can you hear examples of this in the story?

- If it's a casual conversation, you'll often hear people use "fillers" – sounds or words which give them a little time to think. In English, these are things like *um, you know* or *kind of*. Listen to the story and notice when this happens.

- The person telling the story will sometimes mention things which are not very important, before going back to the main points of the story. The word *anyway* is often used to show that the story is going back to what's important. Listen to the story again and see how the speaker does this.

Unit check

1 Fill in the blanks

Complete the text with the words in the box.

| quarrels   wrong   struggled   half-heartedly   ~~important~~   lengths   it's   must   find   couldn't |

I know that it's __important__ to have friends and be nice to them, but I don't always [1] _____ it easy.
A few weeks ago, for example, I was really angry with a friend of mine and shouted at her. Normally, I hate
[2] _____ , and I go to great [3] _____ not to argue, but this time I just [4] _____ avoid it,
especially because I felt that I hadn't done anything [5] _____ . I'd borrowed a DVD from this friend,
and after I'd given it back, she said , "[6] _____ not nice that you scratched my DVD!" She said I
[7] _____ have left it laying around, which of course wasn't true at all. I [8] _____ to keep my
temper, but I didn't succeed, and in the end, we just shouted at each other. The next day, she apologized,
but very [9] _____ , so I didn't really believe her. I guess I need to learn how to deal with people better!

| | 9 |

2 Choose the correct answers

Circle the correct answer: a, b or c.

1 I don't find _____ easy to meet new people.

   a the   b (it)   c them

2 They went to _____ lengths to help me.

   a great   b big   c long

3 Sometimes it can be fun to do things on _____ .

   a mistake   b lengths   c impulse

4 I don't really like dancing, so if I dance at all,
   I dance _____-heartedly.

   a semi   b part   c half

5 You paid $25.00 for this CD? You _____ be crazy!

   a must   b can't   c can

6 _____ I borrow your pen, please?

   a May   b Will   c Should

7 The sky's very dark. I think it _____ rain later this
   afternoon.

   a would   b must   c will

8 I know it's bad news, but I think we _____ tell him
   anyway.

   a should   b would   c can't

9 If you come to Brazil, you _____ come and visit us.
   We'd love to see you!

   a will   b must   c may

| | 8 |

3 Vocabulary

Circle the correct words.

1 She offered to help me, and I'm
   going to *make* / *(seize)* / *struggle* the
   opportunity.

2 I loved math at school. Probably because
   I *made* / *did* / *found* it really easy.

3 Did you say "thank you"? He went to
   great *long* / *problems* / *lengths* to get
   that present for you.

4 Being a nurse doesn't pay a lot, but I get
   a lot out *from* / *of* / *by* helping people.

5 I passed the test easily. It was no
   sweat / *tears* / *difficult*.

6 Thank you for your application. We will
   make every *problem* / *quarrel* / *effort*
   to contact you by the end of the week.

7 You've been sweating *on* / *with* / *over*
   that homework for hours. Take a break.

8 He put everything *on* / *into* / *over*
   making her a birthday card, and she
   didn't even read it.

9 I can't be *worried* / *bothered* / *found*
   to go out tonight. I'm too tired.

| | 8 |

How did you do?

Total: | | 25

| ☺ | Very good 25 – 20 | ☹ | OK 19 – 16 | ☹ | Review Unit 10 again 15 or less |

11 Language

1 Grammar

★ Phrasal verbs

a Match the pictures and the sentences.

1 Should we take off our shoes?
2 You won't get away with this!
3 Let's find out how much that one costs!
4 I wonder what Jenkins has come up with this time.
5 It's awful when they take off.
6 I'm not sure what it is. Why don't you look it up in that book?

b Circle the correct phrasal verb in parentheses. Then complete the sentence with the correct form of the verb.

1 I don't know who did this, but I'm going to _find out_ ! ((find out) / come across)

2 The good weather has _____ an increase in bees this summer. (bring about / take off)

3 How can I _____ it _____ in a dictionary if I don't know how to spell it? (come across / look up)

4 If I were you I would _____ the most expensive one. (come up with / go for)

5 I _____ some old letters from my grandma while I was cleaning the attic. (come across / find out)

6 The plane _____ at four o'clock, so we have to leave by twelve. (take off / go for)

7 She's always late for school, but the teachers never say anything. I don't know how she _____ it! (come up with / get away with)

8 He's _____ a great new idea for cleaning his bedroom quickly. Hide it all under the bed! (come up with / get away with)

c Put the words in order to make sentences or questions.

1 late / plane / the / hours / off / took / two

   The plane took off two hours late.

2 out / I'm / trying / find / to

   _____

3 rude / being / with / away / they / got

   _____

4 the / to / are / dessert / going / you / for / chocolate / go

   _____ ?

5 would / $1,000 / about / problems / an / bring / end / my / to / all

   _____

6 kind / across / comes / as / of / being / superficial / she

   _____

7 means / I / it / know / but / I / what / up, / still / don't / looked / it

   _____

8 that / came / idea / who / with / up / great

   _____ ?

d Rewrite the sentences using *it* or *them* instead of the underlined noun. Change the word order if necessary.

1 She went for <u>the salmon</u>.

She went for it.

2 I never found out <u>the answers to my problems</u>.

_____

3 I came across <u>the coins</u> in my yard.

_____

4 I got away with <u>not doing my homework</u>.

_____

5 I looked up <u>the word</u> in my dictionary.

_____

6 He came up with <u>the idea</u> yesterday.

_____

② Vocabulary

a Complete the sentences with a phrasal verb from the box. Use the correct form of the verb. You may use some of the verbs more than once.

> go for   look up   work out
> come across   take off

1 His plane ___*took off*___ at eleven last night.

2 They were having some problems but things are starting to _____ for them.

3 If we're eating out, I'll always _____ Indian food.

4 It was a great idea, and it _____ immediately.

5 What a lovely bird. Let's _____ it _____ in the guide.

6 I _____ an old book of yours while organizing my bookcase.

7 They _____ as being really unfriendly, but they're just a little shy.

8 Chad _____ his sweater because the room was really hot.

9 The dog really _____ the treats. It likes them a lot.

b (Vocabulary bank) Use the clues to complete the crossword.

Across

1 The language used by deaf people.

3 Very informal language.

5 Words and phrases used by groups of people (scientists, etc.), especially in the workplace.

Down

1 A phrase that is easy to remember, often used in advertising.

2 Terminology that is annoying.

4 An expression that is used very often, so it's not original or interesting.

6 A group of words that has a specific meaning.

③ Pronunciation

Words ending in *-ough*

a Match the words ending in *-ough* and the words they sound like.

-ough sounds		sounds like...	
1 enough	_b_	a blue /u/	
2 through	___	b st<u>u</u>ff /ʌ/	
3 tough	___	c kn<u>ow</u> /oʊ/	
4 cough	___	d <u>o</u>ff /ɔ/	
5 though	___		
6 rough	___		

b ▶ CD4 T22 Listen and check.

c ▶ CD4 T23 Listen and repeat.

1 I didn't have enough money though.

2 That's a nasty cough you've got.

3 This steak is tough all the way through.

4 The ocean isn't rough enough for surfing.

4 Vocabulary

★ Understanding language

a Complete the sentences with the words in the box.

get   out   ~~make~~   lost   gist   totally

1 I can't _make_ out a word of it.

2 Well, I didn't get all of it, but I think I got the _____ .

3 I'm sorry, you _____ me completely at the second "click."

4 Is it just me or is my dad _____ incomprehensible?

5 I can pick _____ a couple of words. This might be "crocodile" but I'm not 100% sure.

6 I don't really _____ it.

b Put the words in order to make sentences.

1 lost / completely / me / he's
   He's completely lost me.

2 understand / to / managing / it / most / I'm / of
   _____
   _____

3 I / the / gist / about / just / can / catch
   _____
   _____

4 saying / I / lot / understand / a / of / what / he's
   _____
   _____

5 can't / I / make / much / very / out
   _____

6 incomprehensible / totally / the / he / gives / are / speeches
   _____
   _____

c Match two of the sentences in Exercise 4b with each of the people in the picture.

1 A might say sentences _____ and _____ .
2 B might say sentences _2_ and _____ .
3 C might say sentences _____ and _____ .

5 Culture in mind

a Rupert Barnes has invented his own language. Read his introduction to it and find out what it's called.

When a student gets frustrated with the oddities and illogicalities of French and German, he or she might give up. Alternatively, he or she might become interested in linguistics. I became interested in linguistics. It has been many years since my schooldays, but I have stayed interested.

Artificial languages are a minor area of linguistics. There are, however, a phenomenal number of artificial languages around. Indeed, while natural languages are shrinking in number, man-made ones are increasing. Of course, there might be just one speaker, or none, of any given man-made tongue.

There are many reasons for someone to want to devise an artificial language, and many people have done so. I have written one myself. I've called it Bannzish. One man might want to find a way for all the peoples of the world to talk together in peace in a common language. For another, it is an intellectual exercise to keep the brain active. Another treats it as an amusement, to fill time. Yet another has it as a way to take his frustrations out on his very words, trying to force an order on them and enjoying some kind of power over them.

My reasons are all of those except the first. The whole idea is ridiculous. Who could think the French would want to abandon the language of Voltaire or the Germans the speech of Goethe? I would certainly not give up the tongue of Shakespeare and Dickens. I have none of those silly delusions which support, for example, Esperanto. Instead I enjoy being pleased with myself for being smart enough to have a good go at the man-made language game. Doing it has also taught me a lot more of depth about the several languages I already knew and brought a new appreciation for English itself.

No exercise like this is ever finished. The English language is still unfinished after 1,500 years of use. I found that I was always coming up with new logical problems and having to think of new subtleties. I am a determined person, and once I started my little intellectual exercise, I could not stop until the end, which never came. Language is not a simple matter. Perhaps the old, illogical, irregular but real languages are better after all. Do not let that stop you from trying the same, though, if you are thinking about it.

b Read the text again and (circle) the correct answer: a, b, c or d.

1 What experience of learning language did the author have at school?
  a He found it boring.
  b He developed a great interest in language which has lasted all his life.
  c He became fluent in both French and German.
  d He only realized how interesting languages were later on in his life.

2 Which of these differences between artificial and natural language does the writer <u>not</u> make?
  a Natural languages are more important.
  b Natural languages are spoken by many more people.
  c The number of natural languages in the world is decreasing.
  d Natural languages are much older than artificial ones.

3 Which of these was not a reason for the author to invent his own language?
  a To try and create a language to bring people together.
  b As an intellectual exercise.
  c For fun.
  d As a way of trying to control language.

4 What is his main criticism of Esperanto?
  a It is designed only for speakers of French and German.
  b It is far too complicated.
  c It is unrealistic and self-important.
  d It isn't well thought-out.

5 What has the writer's experience taught him?
  a It takes a long time to finish a language.
  b No language is perfect.
  c Natural languages are better.
  d Don't waste your time writing an artificial language.

Skills in mind

6 Read

a Read the article and put the paragraphs in order.

☐ Although Sajak and White haven't changed, there have been some changes. In 1987, the shopping was removed and replaced with cash prizes. Later, a bonus round was added. Now the winner gets an additional clue and is given the most common letters in English: R, S, T, L, N and E. The winner guesses three more consonants and one vowel and tries to solve the puzzle. If correct, he or she wins a car or more money. The letters are now displayed on a computer screen. But one thing hasn't changed – *Wheel of Fortune* is a popular hit.

☐ The show was successful during the day from 1975 until 1983. In 1983, the show was aired at night, and it became even more popular. In 1984, it became the number one show on local TV stations in the United States. *Wheel of Fortune* continues to be popular today.

☐ One reason the show is so popular is because of its simplicity. People watching at home can guess the puzzle along with the contestants. The answers are common people, places, things and phrases. For example, *jazz musician*, *busy highway*, *bookmark* and

give me a break. Another reason the show is popular is because of Pat Sajak and Vanna White. Sajak has hosted the show since 1981, and White has been turning the letters since 1982, and audiences love them.

☐ People have been watching the game show *Wheel of Fortune* for several decades, but it wasn't always a success. The show first started in 1973, and it was called *Shopper's Bazaar*. Contestants spun a wheel with dollar amounts on it. Then they guessed letters to solve a puzzle. If they guessed a letter correctly, they got the amount of money on the wheel. At the end of the game, the person with the most money "went shopping" by picking out prizes. The show was not very successful.

☐ Because it wasn't popular, the creator made changes to the show. In 1975, it became *Wheel of Fortune*. A theme was added to the shopping segment for each show. For example, in one show, the winner chose kitchen items and in another show, items used outdoors. The 1975 version of the show was popular on daytime TV.

b Read the text again. Mark the statements *T* (true) or *F* (false). Correct the false statements.

1 *Wheel of Fortune* was first called *Shopper's Bazaar.* [T]

2 In the 1970s, the winner got a cash prize. ☐

3 The show was the number one show in 1975. ☐

4 The puzzles are people, places, things or phrases. ☐

5 Vanna White has been on the show since 1981. ☐

6 Today, the winner gets to "go shopping" if he or she wins the bonus round. ☐

READING TIP

Putting paragraphs in order

● First, read all of the text quickly.

● Next, highlight the first line of each paragraph, which provides a link back to the previous paragraph.

● From your highlighted sentences, find the one which is the beginning of the text as a whole.

● Read the first paragraph carefully and make sure you understand what it is about. Then look at your other first lines. Which one refers back to the topics mentioned in the opening paragraph?

● Repeat this process until you have all the paragraphs in order.

● Finally, read the text carefully using the paragraph order you have chosen. This is your final check to see if it really makes sense.

Unit check

1 Fill in the blanks

Complete the text with the words in the box.

speaks   to speaking   to speak   get   which
incomprehensible   make   ~~language~~   would   learn

English speakers are sometimes said to be the worst ___language___ learners in the world. They think that because everyone else [1]_____ English, they don't need to [2]_____ any other languages. When it comes [3]_____ languages – I'm terrible. In my Japanese classes at school, I [4]_____ spend most of the time trying not to fall asleep. Now I live in Tokyo, and I wish I had paid more attention. When I try [5]_____ Japanese I don't think people can [6]_____ out much of what I say – I'm [7]_____! And when people speak to me, I'm lucky if I can just [8]_____ the gist. Of course, because many people here speak English, they soon start speaking it, [9]_____ means I never practice speaking Japanese!

2 Choose the correct answers

Circle the correct answer: a, b or c.

1   She talks so fast that I can't even _____ the gist.
    a (get)   b find   c see

2   I would _____ for a notebook. They're much easier to carry around with you.
    a select   b choose   c go

3   Many idioms are _____ incomprehensible until you learn what they mean.
    a very   b totally   c such

4   I _____ to pick out a few words.
    a managed   b could   c able

5   He got into trouble for taking _____ his shoes in class.
    a in   b up   c off

6   My younger brother gets _____ with everything. It's not fair.
    a away   b off   c about

7   You've _____ me completely. What exactly are we talking about?
    a caught   b missed   c lost

8   My dad found _____ that I went to the party. He was furious.
    a on   b out   c away

9   I _____ most of what she said but not everything.
    a picked   b understood   c listened   [8]

3 Vocabulary

[9]

Complete the sentences with the missing words. The first letter has been given.

1   My doctor uses so much medical j_a_r_g_o_n, it's difficult to understand him sometimes.

2   Don't talk with food in your mouth. I didn't understand a w_ _ _ _ of what you just said.

3   I_ _ _ _ _ _ are the hardest things to understand. Their meanings are often so different to the words in them.

4   I got the g_ _ _ of what he said, but I didn't understand everything.

5   Be sure to w_ _ _ _ your language when you are around my parents.

6   The teenagers I met in the U.S. spoke so much s_ _ _ _ _ that I couldn't understand them.

7   When we were in Peru, I managed to m_ _ _ out few words of Spanish that I recognized.

8   She's deaf so she uses s_ _ _ _ language to communicate.

9   I got a letter from my lawyer. I don't understand a word of it. It's i_ _ _ _ _ _ _ _ _ _ _ _ _ _ _ _.

[8]

How did you do?

Total: [25]

| ☺ Very good 25 – 20 | 😐 OK 19 – 16 | ☹ Review Unit 11 again 15 or less |

12 Using fame to help

1 Grammar

✱ Reduced relative clauses

a Read the text. At the end of each line, write a check (✓) if the underlined words are needed or write an *X* if the underlined words are not needed.

Roger Federer, [1]who is a top *ATP player and a strong supporter of children's charities, became a UNICEF Goodwill Ambassador in April 2006. Like other Goodwill Ambassadors such as David Beckham and Youssou N'dour, Federer will work to support UNICEF in its efforts to bring attention and resources to children around the world [2]who need help.

1	**X**
2	....

"I am happy to become one of UNICEF's Goodwill Ambassadors," Federer said. "I've been lucky in life, and able to play tennis seriously since I was six years old. It's important to me to help the many children throughout the world [3]who do not have the everyday things they need."

3	....

Federer has used his success in tennis to remind the world that children are important. In 2003, he started the Roger Federer Foundation, [4]which raises money for disadvantaged children, mainly in South Africa (where his mother was brought up), and to promote sports for young people.

4	....

After the terrible tsunami of 2004, Federer started several fund-raising campaigns, including the ATP All-Star Rally for Relief, a tennis event [5]which was supported by many of the top men and women players. All the money [6]that was raised went to UNICEF.

5	....
6	....

That event started a worldwide partnership between the ATP and UNICEF called ACE (Assisting Children Everywhere), [7]which aims to use the power of tennis to help provide health, education and protection to the poor children of the world.

7	....

*ATP = Association of Tennis Professionals

b In each sentence, write ↑ in the place where the relative pronoun and the verb are missing. Then write *which* or *who* and the correct verb in the blank.

1 Coldplay performed a song ↑ called "Violet Hill". _____*which was*_____

2 Here is an extract taken from the first chapter of the book. _____

3 The Great Sphinx is a famous statue, half-human, half-lion, built by the Egyptians.

   _____

4 Harry Potter is a fictional character created by J. K. Rowling. _____

5 The A380 plane, built by Airbus Industries, can seat over 550 passengers.

   _____

6 The Live 8 concert attended by 15,000 people was a success. _____

2 Vocabulary

✱ Fame

a Circle the correct words: a, b or c.

1 He's famous _____ making fun of politicians.
   a from   b (for)   c by

2 Some people _____ a name for themselves by doing crazy things.
   a have   b do   c make

3 Her career started slowly, but then she really _____ it big in 2010.
   a made   b did   c had

4 Roger Federer is such a successful tennis player that now he's a _____ name.
   a house   b home   c household

5 Not many people know her now, but she _____ a lot of success back in the 1990s.
   a made   b enjoyed   c liked

6 Justin Bieber became a singing _____ a few years ago.
   a sensation   b sense   c excitement

b Complete the text with words from Exercise 2a.

John McEnroe

John McEnroe was an American tennis player in the 1980s and 1990s who became famous _for_ shouting at umpires and throwing his racket around. Born in 1959, he was a teenage tennis ¹ .... who won the French junior championship at the age of 18. Later in 1977, he reached the semi-finals at Wimbledon and became a ² .... name all over the world. He really ³ .... it big in 1979 when he won the US Open title in front of his home crowd. By that time, he had also ⁴ .... a name for himself as a player who regularly lost his temper and shouted at opponents and officials. His most famous phrase was "You cannot be serious!"

After he retired from playing tennis in 1992, McEnroe ⁵ .... a lot of success as a TV tennis commentator.

3 Vocabulary
✱ Expressing opinions

a Complete the sentences with the words in the box.

> thought   seems   concerned
> ask   way   ~~opinion~~

1 In my _opinion_ , celebrities should stay out of politics.

2 I'd have .... that movie stars could really help with world problems.

3 The .... I see it, poor people need help from anywhere in the world.

4 As far as I'm .... , the celebrities just want publicity for themselves.

5 It .... to me that celebrities should do all they can for charities.

6 If you .... me, soccer players are the best Goodwill Ambassadors.

b Put the words in the correct order to make expressions that give opinions.

1 for / I'm / all / it   ☑
   I'm all for it.

2 less / care / couldn't / I   ☐
   ....

3 matter / it / really / doesn't   ☐
   ....

4 not / it's / a / idea / good   ☐
   ....

5 against / completely / I'm / it   ☐
   ....

6 thing / it / be / can't / a / bad   ☐
   ....

c Next to each expression in Exercise 3b, write a check (✓) if it gives a positive opinion, write an X if it gives a negative opinion, or Ø if it gives a neutral opinion.

d **Vocabulary bank** Complete the sentences with the words in the box.

> express   high   difference   public
> ~~matter~~   poll   humble   second

1 It depends on who you talk to. It's a _matter_ of opinion, really.

2 It's unusual for Jack not to say anything. He usually loves to .... his opinion.

3 I've thought long and hard about your proposal and it's my .... opinion that we should do it.

4 Let's not argue. Let's agree that we have a .... of opinion.

5 If you're not happy with what the doctor said, you should definitely get a .... opinion.

6 Lucy thinks she's so great. She has such a .... opinion of herself.

7 The government doesn't have a chance in the elections if you believe the latest opinion ....

8 The government wants to go to war even though .... opinion is against it.

4 Grammar

★ Tag questions review

a Some of these tag questions are incorrect. If the tag question is correct, write a check (✓). If the tag question is incorrect, write an X and the correct tag question.

1 It's an important issue, isn't it? ✓

2 Harry Potter's known all over the world, aren't they? ✗ _isn't he?_

3 You aren't sure what to do, do you? ☐
....

4 Angelina Jolie works for UNICEF, don't she?
☐ ....

5 He went to Africa to see the problem, hasn't he?
☐ ....

6 She can act very well, can't she? ☐
....

7 The movie didn't do very well, didn't it? ☐
....

8 They enjoyed a lot of success in the 1990s, weren't they? ☐ ....

9 He's really made a name for himself, hasn't he?
☐ ....

10 They couldn't raise enough money, could they?
☐ ....

b Complete the sentences with the correct tag questions.

1 They don't help out very much, _do they?_

2 It's boring to read about all these movie stars,
.... ?

3 They haven't enjoyed much success,
.... ?

4 She doesn't mind being famous,
.... ?

5 She'll do anything to get more publicity,
.... ?

6 They tried everything they could to help,
.... ?

7 We should try to raise money for them,
.... ?

8 They couldn't get help to all the starving people,
.... ?

c Complete the dialogue with the correct tag questions.

David: Did you see the show about celebrity charity work last night?

Carol: Yes, it was interesting,
[1] _wasn't it?_

David: Not really. It didn't tell you much you didn't already know,
[2] .... ?

Carol: What do you mean?

David: I mean, we already know everything there is to know about Brad Pitt, [3] .... ? People don't want to see his face on TV again,
[4] .... ?

Carol: Oh, David, you can be really boring sometimes.

David: Sorry, but you asked me what I thought.

Carol: Well, yes – but if you always talk like that, people won't ask you for your opinion very often, [5] .... ?

David: OK, I'm sorry. Let's talk about something else.

Carol: But David, you don't really think charity work is silly, [6] .... ?

d ▶ CD4 T24 Listen and check.

5 Pronunciation

✱ Intonation in tag questions

a ▶ CD4 T24 Listen to the dialogue in Exercise 4c again. In one of the tag questions, the voice goes up at the end – which one is it?

b ▶ CD4 T25 Listen to the sentences. For each one, write ↑ if the person is asking a question to check information (the voice goes up at the end), or ↓ if the person is just trying to start a conversation (the voice goes down at the end).

1 You're new here, aren't you?   ↓

2 You speak French, don't you?   ↑

3 I'm being boring, aren't I? _____

4 It was an interesting show, wasn't it? _____

5 You didn't enjoy it very much, did you? _____

6 This is a great party, isn't it? _____

7 They won't be late, will they? _____

8 You don't like this kind of music, do you? _____

c ▶ CD4 T25 Listen again and repeat.

6 Everyday English

a Put the words in order to make phrases.

1 bet / I _____I bet_____

2 well / as / might / we

_____

3 it / forget _____

4 out / it / cut _____

5 less / I / care / couldn't

_____

6 much / I / as / thought

_____

b Which of the expressions in Exercise 6a means ...

a Don't worry about it.   _3_

b Can you stop doing (or saying) that? _____

c I can't see any reason why we shouldn't. _____

d I'm certain. _____

e I really don't have an opinion about that. _____

f That doesn't surprise me. _____

c Complete the dialogue. with the expressions in Exercise 6a.

Lucy: Have you heard that Mark Smith is going to release a book about his life in politics?

Ollie: ¹ _____ . I mean, I can't think of anything less interesting.

Lucy: Really? I think it's pretty exciting. He promises that he's going to paint a picture of what life is really like when you're the mayor of a big city.

Ollie: ² _____ he doesn't say anything that we don't already know.

Lucy: Well, perhaps you should read the book before you express your opinion about it.

Ollie: I don't need to. These politicians are all the same. They're only interested in talking about themselves. They don't really care about us.

Lucy: ³ _____ , Ollie. He was a good mayor, and he has done a lot of good around the world since he retired. In fact, he's giving all the money he makes from the book to help education in Africa.

Ollie: Well, he doesn't need it. I mean, he's not exactly short of money. If he sold some of the houses he owns or gave half his salary to charity, I might be impressed. He's just using his charity work to keep himself in the public eye. In case we forget about him.

Lucy: Wow, you're really not a fan of his, are you?

Ollie: No, not really.

Lucy: ⁴ _____ .

Ollie: Well, when you've read the book, maybe you can persuade me otherwise.

Lucy: ⁵ _____ I don't think I can be bothered.

Ollie: You're right. We always disagree, so ⁶ _____ not talk about politics any more.

Lucy: Good idea.

7 Listen

a ▶ **CD4 T26** Listen to an interview with an expert about UNICEF. Mark the statements *T* (true) or *F* (false).

1 UNICEF's ambassadors include photographers. `T`

2 A Goodwill Ambassador's commitment begins when he or she starts working for UNICEF.

3 Youssou N'Dour became an ambassador in 1987.

4 Shakira had already worked in the area of children's education.

5 The two important things about ambassadors are: they get attention and they make decisions.

6 UNICEF wants children to have health, education, equality and protection.

7 Danny Kaye became Ambassador at Large in 1954.

8 Audrey Hepburn was also Ambassador at Large.

b ▶ **CD4 T26** Listen again and answer the questions.

1 What do all UNICEF's celebrities share?

....

....

2 Before he became a UNICEF ambassador, Youssou N'Dour took part in an immunization program. What else did he do?

....

....

3 Why is it important that UNICEF's ambassadors have access to politicians?

....

....

4 Why do politicians sometimes not pay much attention to children?

....

....

EXAM TIP

Before you listen and do a task

- Good preparation is very important, especially for a listening task. You might not have time to read all the questions before you listen. But try to read and really think about as many of the questions as possible.

- With true / false tasks, like in Exercise 6a, read each sentence and consider what could be true or false about it. Key words will help you.

- With open-ended questions, like in Exercise 6b, read and again decide what the key words are. For example, in the first sentence, the key words are *celebrities* and *share*. You might not hear these exact words when you listen: what other words might you hear?

Unit check

1 Fill in the blanks

Complete the text with the words in the box.

> will   won't   ~~myself~~   see   concerned
> enjoying   bad   make   big   household

I've always dreamed of making a real name for ___myself___ in the music industry. I decided I'd make it
¹ _____ with a guitar I borrowed from a friend. My friend said, "I really love that guitar, so you'll
give it back to me, ² _____ you?" "Sure," I said. "When I ³ _____ it big, I'll give it back to you!"
He looked a little worried. "Look," I said, "the way I ⁴ _____ it, in a year or two I'm going to be a
⁵ _____ name! I'm going to be rich! Then I'll buy you all the guitars you want."

"Well," he said, "I guess that can't be a ⁶ _____ thing. But listen – when you're ⁷ _____ all that
success, you won't forget that I helped you, ⁸ _____ you?"

"It's OK, Jack," I replied. "As far as I'm ⁹ _____ , you're the best friend I've ever had, and of course
I won't forget you." He looked me in the eye. "My name isn't Jack – it's Joe!" He took the guitar back,
and that was the end of my musical career.

9

2 Choose the correct answers

Circle the correct answer: a, b or c.

1 They really _____ in 2003 with their first CD.
   a made it large   **b (made it big)**   c did it big

2 You won't tell anyone, _____ you?
   a will   b won't   c shall

3 They didn't _____ a lot of success with their
   last album.
   a make   b win   c enjoy

4 A vacation in Thailand? I'm all _____ it!
   a with   b on   c for

5 He hasn't called you, _____ he?
   a had   b hasn't   c has

6 It _____ to me that UNICEF does great work
   all over the world.
   a seems   b view   c thought

7 The weren't very famous, _____ they?
   a are   b were   c weren't

8 I'd have _____ that the money could be spent
   in better ways.
   a concerned   b asked   c thought

9 They didn't pay you, _____ they?
   a do   b did   c didn't

8

3 Vocabulary

Change the underlined words. Use the
words in parentheses.

1 It seems to me they got what
   they deserved. **(concerned)**
   As far as I'm concerned

2 He became famous by winning
   a reality TV show. **(name)**
   _____

3 They didn't agree. **(difference)**
   _____

4 Why don't you ask another
   doctor what he thinks? **(second)**
   _____

5 If you ask me, they were both wrong.
   (way) _____

6 He really does think he's great. **(high)**
   _____

7 Everyone knows him. **(household)**
   _____

8 He became successful in Japan. **(big)**
   _____

9 He was very successful for a few years.
   (enjoyed) _____

8

How did you do?

Total: [25]

| ☺ Very good 25 – 20 | 😐 OK 19 – 16 | ☹ Review Unit 12 again 15 or less |

Music is everywhere.

1 Grammar

✳ Indirect questions

a Put the words in the correct order to make indirect questions.

1 you / can / where / find / post office / out / is / the

   Can you find out where the post office is?

2 don't / much / costs / I / how / this / know

   ....

3 no / we / starts / have / what / movie / idea / the / time

   ....

4 like / I'd / know / test / he / what / grade / got / to / on / the

   ....

5 arrived / you / when / find / can / they / out

   .... ?

6 speak / wonder / can / if / I / I / to / him

   ....

7 you / why / teacher / could / isn't / ask / here / the

   .... ?

8 is / you / name / what / out / can / his / find

   .... ?

b Write the indirect questions in Exercise 1a as direct questions.

1 *Where is the post office?*

2 ....

3 ....

4 ....

5 ....

6 ....

7 ....

8 ....

c Anne Jacobs has an unusual job. She is responsible for choosing the music to play at Globo Gym. Read the interview with her and match the questions with the replies.

1 What kind of music do you play at the gym? [f]

2 What type of music is popular in the early mornings, for example? [ ]

3 What did you play this morning when you opened the gym? [ ]

4 What do people like to listen to while they exercise in the afternoons? [ ]

5 What time does it start getting busy again? [ ]

6 And what kind of music can we hear then? [ ]

7 How many clients does the gym have right now? [ ]

8 And how many complaints have you had about the music you play? [ ]

a None, incredibly. I guess I must be doing something right.

b Well, that's usually our busiest time, so something upbeat is good to get our clients moving and ready for the working day.

c Let me see. Yes, I remember. It was a collection of remixed songs by Madonna, Girls Aloud and people like that.

d The gym starts filling up around 6:00 p.m. with people dropping in on their way home from work.

e Over 500, I think.

f All types. It depends on the time of the day.

g After lunch is our quietest time of the day, so we usually play slower, more relaxing music. "Chill out" music, for example.

h Rock's pretty popular in the early evening. It helps people get in the mood for a night out.

d Make the questions in Exercise 1c indirect questions.

1 I wonder   *what kind of music you play at the gym.*

2 I wonder _____ .

3 I don't know _____ .
_____

4 I'd like to know _____ .
_____

5 I wonder _____ .
_____

6 I don't know _____ .
_____

7 Can you find out _____ ?
_____

8 Can you find out _____ ?
_____

2 Vocabulary

✱ Qualifying comparisons

a Jenny saw several bands at a music festival. Put the bands she mentions in order of who she liked most.

"**The White Stripes** were a little better than **Fatboy Slim**, but not much."

"**Keane** was almost as good as **Coldplay**, but neither were as good as **Elvis Costello**."

"Although **Echo and the Bunnymen** are a big influence on Coldplay, Coldplay was far better. Echo and the Bunnymen were a lot better than the other 80s band, **New Order**."

"**The Magic Numbers** were the best. They were just fantastic."

"Fatboy Slim and the White Stripes were nowhere near as good as the other bands."

1 *The Magic Numbers*

2 _____

3 _____

4 _____

5 _____

6 _____

7 _____

8 _____

b Complete the sentences w~~ith~~ words in the box.

> just   nowhere   almost   ne~~ar~~
> far   better   ~~more~~   even

1 I find classical music much   *more*   relaxing than any pop music.

2 Music these days is nowhere _____ as imaginative as it was 20 years ago.

3 I think rap is _____ as good as hip-hop. I think hip-hop is a little better.

4 Country music is _____ as boring as folk music. I don't really like either.

5 The Beatles are _____ better than Oasis. I don't know how you can compare them.

6 Bands' images are _____ more important than their music these days. It's a shame.

7 Pop music is _____ near as good as jazz.

8 The live version of this song is even _____ than the studio version.

3 Pronunciation

✱ *record* (noun) vs. *record* (verb)

a ▶ CD4 T27   Listen and mark the stress on the words in italics.

1 We *export* a lot of coffee to Europe.

2 Sugar is our biggest *export*.

3 There's been an *increase* in car theft recently.

4 The graph shows that the number of university students *increases* every year.

5 I'm sorry. I didn't mean to *insult* you.

6 Don't do that with your hand. It's considered an *insult* here.

7 What a nice *present*. Thank you.

8 We'd like to *present* you with the "Student of the Month" certificate.

b ▶ CD4 T27   Listen again and repeat.

4 Vocabulary

✶ Listening to music

a What are the words? Complete the sentences.

1 I love dance music – anything with a good _beat_ (tabe) to it.

2 Most .... (scirly) these days are kind of silly, but occasionally you get a songwriter with something to say.

3 Living in a small town, we don't get much .... (vile) music, we only get a couple of shows a year if we're lucky.

4 It's a great .... (neut). It's so easy to sing along to.

5 I don't have a great voice, so I tend not to sing. I just .... (muh) along.

6 We .... (decorred) our first CD in my dad's garage in three days.

7 .... (unranmtliest) music is great to play in the background when you're working.

b **Vocabulary bank** Complete the text with the words in the box. There are two you won't need.

> album   track   soundtrack   label   elevator music   cover   cover band   compose   singer-songwriter

They say that a change is as good as a rest, and this certainly seems true for Ricky Valentine. When he left Sony Music two years ago to sign for a small independent record _label_ , many people were predicting we'd heard the last from him. But this is not the case. His first [1] .... for Go-Go Records is incredible. *Back from the Dead* shows that Valentine is not just a great [2] .... (we all knew that anyway) but that he can [3] .... music on a much more ambitious level. This is not just a record of Valentine and his guitar. This is Valentine, his guitar and a full orchestra. At times you feel like you're listening to the [4] .... of some epic Hollywood production. It's pretty amazing and quite unlike anything he's done before. The opening [5] .... , which is a [6] .... of U2's "One", is mind-blowing. The rest of the songs (all original compositions) don't disappoint. If you only buy one CD this year, makes sure it's this one.

5 Grammar

✶ verbs + *wh*- clauses

a Complete the sentences with the correct question word, *who, when, why, where, what* or *how*.

1 I can't imagine _who_ told him.

2 I've forgotten .... her birthday is.

3 I wonder .... much it costs.

4 He didn't say .... he lives.

5 I don't know .... she didn't call to say "happy birthday."

6 I don't understand .... she likes about him.

b Match the two parts of the sentences. Then add question marks or periods.

1 It's easy to

2 Can you tell

3 Who told you

4 I'm thinking about where I want

5 Why didn't you

6 I don't know where

7 I don't understand

8 Do you

a how it works ....

b they went ....

c me why he did that ....

d come to my party last week ....

e know where he went ....

f to go on vacation this year ....

g see why he's so happy ....

h where I live ....

6 Fiction in mind

a Read this extract from *High Fidelity* by Nick Hornby. These statements are all true. Find evidence for each one in the text. There might be more than one thing for each statement.

1 Rob has been a DJ at the club before.
2 Rob doesn't think that Barry's band will be good.
3 Barry and his band are very good.
4 The people in the club are not teenagers.

Rob, the owner of the music store, is working one night as DJ in a nightclub. Barry, who works in Rob's store, has a band which is going to play in public for the first time at the club.

Before the band comes on, everything's great. It used to take a bit of time to warm people up, but tonight they're ¹ <u>up for it</u> right away.

[And] I haven't lost any of the old magic. One sequence [of songs] has them begging for mercy. And then it's time for the band.

I've been told to introduce them; Barry has even written down what I'm supposed to say: "Ladies and gentlemen, be afraid. Be very afraid. Here comes … SONIC DEATH MONKEY!" But […] in the end I just sort of mumble the name of the group into the microphone.

They're wearing suits and skinny ties, and when they plug in there's a terrible feedback ² <u>whine</u> which for a moment I fear is their opening number. But Sonic Death Monkey are no longer what they once were. They are no longer, in fact, Sonic Death Monkey.

"We're not called Sonic Death Monkey any more," Barry says when he gets to the mike. "We might be on the edge of becoming the Futuristics, but we haven't decided yet. Tonight, though, we're Backbeat. One two three … WELL SHAKE IT UP BABY …" And they launch into "Twist and Shout," note perfect, and everyone in the place goes mad.

And Barry can sing.

They play "Route 66" and "Long Tall Sally" and "Money" and "Do You Love Me?" and they ³ <u>encore</u> with "In the Midnight Hour" and "La Bamba". Every song, in short, is ⁴ <u>naff</u> and recognizable, and guaranteed to please a crowd of thirtysomethings who think that hip-hop is something their children do in music and movement classes. The crowd is so pleased, in fact, that they ⁵ <u>sit out</u> the songs I have lined up for them to get them going again after Sonic Death Monkey have frightened and confused them.

"What was all that about?" I ask Barry when he comes up to the deck, sweaty […] and pleased with himself.

"Was that all right?"

"It was better than what I was expecting."

b (Circle) the word or phrase which is closest in meaning to the <u>underlined</u> words in the text.

1 a trying to leave   b enthusiastic   c cold
2 a something to drink   b an electric shock   c an unpleasant high sound
3 a play extra songs   b play badly   c play the same songs again
4 a unknown   b badly sung   c old, outdated
5 a don't like   b don't dance to   c go outside to sit down

c Answer the questions.

1 What is "the old magic" that Rob says he hasn't lost?
2 Why does Rob "just sort of mumble the name of the group" when he introduces them?
3 What does the crowd think of the songs Rob plays when the band has finished?
4 What, in your opinion, does Rob feel about the evening at the club?

Skills in mind

7 Write

a Read the concert review and <u>underline</u> the names of:

1 the two bands that played

2 two members of the main band

3 five songs that they played

CONCERTS – *Rolling Stones Special*

Fenway Park doesn't see many rock concerts. It's in a residential area and can't hold loud concerts late at night, for example. It seemed strange then, that the Rolling Stones chose this place in Boston to start the tour for their CD, *A Bigger Bang.* **A** ☐ Indeed, city workers were there to measure sound levels. If the "bang" was "bigger" than 73 decibels, then it would have to be turned down.

Luckily, that wasn't necessary – although it might have been fun to see an official walk on stage to tell Keith Richards and the band to keep quiet. Imagine what the reaction would have been from the thousands of fans who had waited in line for hours to get into the stadium. Not nearly as polite as it was for the Black Eyed Peas, who played enthusiastic and energetic opening songs, I'm sure. While the Black Eyed Peas did their best, it was clear who everyone was waiting for.

Just after eight, a huge roar erupted as the Stones began their show with "Start Me Up." The crowd went wild. Five songs into the show and the band introduced "Rough Justice," the first of several songs on the CD. I thought the song was amazing. **B** ☐

As the show continued with the band playing a mixture of old and new, I had to admire the energy of these men, who are all in their sixties now. Amazingly, they sounded just as young and fresh as they did twenty years ago. Mick Jagger was pretty amazing. **C** ☐1☐

Then, while the band was playing "Miss You," the huge stage opened up and a mini-stage came out, taking the band into the heart of the audience. It was here that they played the best song of the night, "Satisfaction." **D** ☐ Each song that Mick Jagger and the band played was accompanied by amazing special effects.

The lively "Jumping Jack Flash" made sure the show finished on a high note while the encores "You Can't Always Get What You Want" and "It's Only Rock 'n' Roll" sent the crowd home singing happily. This might have been the opening night, but the band couldn't have sounded more professional. **E** ☐ It looks like the Stones are going to be popular for a long time.

b Read the text again and add the sentences. Write 1–6 in the boxes A–E. There is one sentence that you won't need.

1 No one knows better than him how to entertain.

2 The song would have taken the roof off the stadium, if it had had one.

3 Apparently they rehearsed for weeks for this tour, and it showed.

4 Their music has taken the Stones all over the world.

5 They are, after all, a band that likes to rock and roll as loud as possible.

6 And from their reaction, I think the crowd agreed with me.

c Write a review (200–250 words) of a performance you've seen either live or on TV.

EXAM TIP

Justifying an opinion

● When you give an opinion in your writing, always write a supporting sentence to back it up. This will make your opinion sound more interesting.

● Look at Exercise 7b again. All the sentences that you added into the text support the writer's opinions. With these sentences, the text is more effective.

Unit check

1 Fill in the blanks

Complete the text with the words in the box.

album almost ~~band~~ live far guitar musical record recorded talented

Tegan and Sara is an indie ____band____ from Canada. The band gets its name from its two members: Tegan and Sara Quin. They are twin sisters. Both sisters sing and play the [1] _____ . Their [2] _____ style is considered folk-rock or indie-pop. They became successful by winning a competition in Canada in 1998 with the highest score in the history of the competition. They began touring with the Lilith Fair, which is a [3] _____ concert that travels throughout Canada and the United States. The musicians are all [4] _____ women, and the money raised goes to charity. Tegan and Sara's first [5] _____ , called *Under Feet Like Ours*, was released independently. Their second album, *The Business of Art*, was released with a [6] _____ label. Since then, they have [7] _____ and released four more albums. Their last two albums have had [8] _____ more success than the previous ones. They have been [9] _____ as popular in the U.S. as they are in Canada.

| 9 |

2 Choose the correct answers

Circle the correct answer: a, b or c.

1 Do you know how _____ ?
   a old is she b old her is c (old she is)

2 Their new CD is _____ as good as their first one.
   a nowhere b far c almost

3 What an annoying tune! I just can't get it out of my _____ .
   a head b mouth c ears

4 Can you find out what language _____ in Brazil?
   a they speak b speak they c do they speak

5 My dad thinks he's really cool singing _____ to my music. I think it's embarrassing.
   a on b along c out

6 I'd like to know what _____ .
   a did he say b he said c said he

7 It's _____ as hot today as it was yesterday.
   a far b just c even

8 I have no idea what _____ .
   a said he b did he say c he said

9 If you forget the words, just _____ along.
   a hum b sing c yawn

| 8 |

3 Vocabulary

Underline the correct word.

1 He's nowhere *far / close / near* as famous as his brother.

2 It's so embarrassing when my mom sings *along / though / on* to songs on the radio.

3 I love *alive / live / life* music. I go to at least two concerts a month.

4 I used to work in a mall, but the *track / stairs / elevator* music they played all day drove me crazy.

5 My brother's band has just signed to a big record *sign / label / brand*.

6 This CD is *even / just / near* better than their last CD.

7 The *words / tune / track* is easy to remember, but the lyrics are difficult.

8 I'm in a band that mainly plays *cover / copy / fake* versions of famous songs.

9 I can't choose between them. I think they're *just / even / the same* as good as each other.

| 8 |

How did you do?

Total: | 25 |

| 😊 | Very good
25 – 20 | 😐 | OK
19 – 16 | 😞 | Review Unit 13 again
15 or less |

Nature's best

① Grammar

❋ Participial phrases

a Check (✓) the sentences where the subject of the participial phrase is the same as the subject of the main clause.

1 Watching the late-night movie on TV, we fell asleep. ✓

2 Walking down the road, the sun was shining. ....

3 Sitting in a chair, the book was very interesting. ....

4 Having seen the movie, I decided not to go to the theater. ....

5 Having arrived two hours early, I had to wait at the airport. ....

6 Knowing no one there, the party was kind of boring. ....

7 Having heard a strange noise in the kitchen, I went to investigate. ....

b Rewrite the underlined sentences to make five new sentences using participial phrases.

¹I'm looking out over Guanabara Bay and I can't imagine anywhere else I'd rather be. Sugar Loaf Mountain rises out of the ocean at an impossible angle. You have to see it to believe it. ²The city of Rio de Janeiro hugs the hillsides behind me. It's one of the most beautiful places I've ever seen. Sand, sea and nightlife – I think I'm really going to enjoy this week of my South American adventure. We arrived here yesterday morning. ³We checked into a cheap hotel in the Glória district and then made our way immediately to the beach. We stayed there the whole day. ⁴Dave spent all day in the sun, and then he spent all night complaining about his sunburn. Of course, I was more sensible. ⁵I rented a chair and an umbrella on the beach and spent most of the time reading my Rio de Janeiro guide. I found out that this whole area was discovered by the Portuguese, which is why Brazilians today don't speak Spanish like the rest of South America.

1 *Looking out over Guanabara Bay, I can't imagine anywhere else I'd rather be.* ....

2 ....

3 ....

4 ....

5 ....

2 Vocabulary

★ Geographical features

a Complete the sentences with the words in the box. There are three that you won't use.

> glacier   lake   cliffs   ~~coral reef~~   plain   desert   mountain range   bay   canyon

1 The Great Barrier *__coral reef__* is off the coast of *Australia / New Zealand.*

2 _____ Titicaca is in *Bolivia and Peru / Mexico and the U.S.*

3 The Grand _____ is in *the U.S. / Mexico.*

4 The Andes _____ is in *South America / Europe.*

5 The white _____ of Dover are on the coast of *Ireland / England.*

6 The Gobi _____ is in *China /Japan.*

b Now <u>underline</u> the correct country/countries to make the sentences true.

3 Grammar

★ Passive of *need to* and *have to*

a Which sentence matches the picture best? Write *a* or *b*.

a "I need to buy a bus ticket."
b "A bus ticket needs to be bought."

a "I have to fix my computer."
b "My computer has to be fixed."

a "You have to check your ticket."
b "Your bag has to be checked."

a "I need to clean my clothes."
b "My clothes need to be cleaned."

a "We need to climb up there to see the view."
b "This mountain needs to be climbed."

a "I have to pass this test."
b "I have to be tested next week."

b Complete the sentences. Use the simple present form of the verbs in parentheses and *to be* plus past participle.

1 Your bicycle *__has to be checked__* (have/check) before you ride in the competition.

2 Your application _____ (need/complete).

3 Your number _____ (has/attach) to your shirt.

4 The spectators _____ (need/tell) where to stand.

5 The race _____ (has/do) by dark.

4 Vocabulary

✳ Travel verbs

a Complete the story with the prepositions in the box. You will use some more than once.

> for   on   to   back   out   away   off   in

All I wanted was to get _____back_____ home. I had been ¹ _____ for two weeks, acting in a play at the Swan Theater in Stratford. Now I was tired, and I had a big bag of laundry to do! Besides, a group of friends from school and I were all going ² _____ vacation the next day. We were going ³ _____ the ferry to the Toronto Islands, and we were all really excited. My parents had bought me a ticket so that I could fly home to Toronto, to save time. I got ⁴ _____ the airport at 1:00 p.m. My flight took ⁵ _____ at 3:00 p.m., so I had plenty of time. When I got to the gate, I learned my flight had been delayed an hour. An hour was no big deal, so I went ⁶ _____ a walk around the airport. When I got back, I found out my flight had been cancelled all together. In fact, all flights to Toronto had been cancelled for the rest of the day. I couldn't waste a minute. I ran

out of the airport and got ⁷ _____ a taxi. "Stratford train station quickly, please!" I told the man. We set ⁸ _____ immediately. "Good," I thought. There was only one problem. The taxi driver was new to the job and got completely lost in Stratford. An hour and a half later, I finally got ⁹ _____ of the taxi and ran into the station. I was in luck. There was a train leaving ¹⁰ _____ Toronto in ten minutes. It was the last one of the day, and I was going to get home! I got ¹¹ _____ the train, found my seat, sat down and fell asleep. The next thing I knew, someone was talking to me loudly. I woke up with a start. It was the train agent. "Time to get ¹² _____ the train, young man," he said. "What?" I replied. "Are we in Toronto already?" "Toronto?" he said. "We're in Kingston. We passed Toronto about two and a half hours ago."

b **Vocabulary bank** (Circle) the best options.

1 We're going on a school (excursion) / expedition to Quebec on Monday.

2 My mother's on a business *trip* / *tour* in Quito until Friday.

3 Next year Mom and Dad are taking us on a five-week *tour* / *trip* around the United States. I can't wait.

4 We're flying to Sydney with an overnight *excursion* / *layover* in Singapore.

5 My grandma lives on the coast in Chile. It's a ten-hour *commute* / *journey* to get there.

6 I have to *commute* / *backpack* two hours to work every day.

7 I'd hate to go on a *cruise* / *journey*. Two weeks on a ship? I'd go crazy!

8 Their jungle *expedition* / *voyage* was a disaster, and they had to return home after only three days.

5 Pronunciation

✳ /ɪ/ s*i*t and /i/ s*ea*t

a ▶ **CD4 T28** Listen and (circle) the words you hear.

1 She *beat* / (bit) into her sandwich.

2 I'll *heat* / *hit* the chicken.

3 Can you *feel* / *fill* it?

4 The *sheep* / *ship* is leaving in the morning.

5 The *peel* / *pill* is thick and orange.

6 Where did you put the *beans* / *bins*?

7 Did he *leave* / *live* in the car?

8 Don't *sleep* / *slip*!

b ▶ **CD4 T28** Listen again and repeat.

6 Read

a Read the text. Complete the sentences with one word in each blank. There is often more than one possibility.

Over the last two hundred years, a lot of music has been ___written___ which tries to create, in sound, an emotionally charged picture of the natural world. Think of Vivaldi's *The Four Seasons* or Beethoven's *Pastoral Symphony*, to name only the ¹ _____ famous.

One way in ² _____ composers create these pictures is through imitating natural sounds. People have long recognized that humans are not the only creatures that make music. Birdsong is the most obvious ³ _____ of non-human music that composers have tried to recreate.

Perhaps the most bizarre musical collaboration ⁴ _____ humans and birds occurred in 1717, when *The Bird Fancyer's Delight* was published. This gave a selection of simple tunes which ⁵ _____ be played on a recorder to caged songbirds until the birds themselves learned them by ⁶ _____ . Then you could sit back and listen to your pet canary chirp to the latest popular tune! However, if you wanted a bird to ⁷ _____ a more complex tune then, as *The Bird Fancyer's Delight* tells us, you had to spend hours playing music to it in a dark room.

And it's not just birds, of course, that "sing." Recordings of whales "singing" have been very popular in ⁸ _____ years. In China, some people keep caged cicadas ⁹ _____ of birds, because of the "music" that they make!

Are the sounds made by animals just an expression of their feelings or instincts? Can we really ¹⁰ _____ these sounds music? Biologists tell us that a robin singing in a tree is in fact claiming territory and warning other males to ¹¹ _____ clear. It's hardly the equivalent of a song by Schubert, is it?

b ▶ CD4 T29 Listen and complete the album titles.

1 Pacific ___Blue___

2 Coral _____

3 Classical _____

4 Eternal _____

c ▶ CD4 T29 Listen again and answer the questions.

Which CD ...

1 promises inspiration? __3__

2 features two very different musical instruments? _____

3 features two different types of water sounds? _____

4 mixes animal noises and human voices? _____

5 mixes the sounds of two different animals? _____

6 includes classical music? _____

7 ## Listen

▶ **CD4 T30** Listen and complete the news report about vacation destinations and activities with a word or a number.

Beautiful Beaches

In our special beach survey we found that the beach is still the top vacation destination for Americans. Of the more than ¹........................ people who answered our questionnaire, ²........................% said they would "definitely" or "very likely" pay a visit to the beach sometime in the next year. And ³........................% chose the beach as the perfect place for taking a vacation.

And what will they do when they get there? The top answer was have a party or a barbecue, while only 68% said they will swim in the ocean. Another 27% said they would get their ⁴........................ wet, leaving 5% with no intention of getting in the water at all. Perhaps it's the thought of all those jellyfish, which just beat sharks as the nation's biggest fear about the ocean.

Top five things to do on the beach

1	Have a party / barbecue	44%
2	Build a ⁵........................	39%
3	Relax with a book	32%
4	Hang out with ⁶........................	21%
5	Fly a kite	⁷........%

Things to keep you out of the water

Thirty-nine percent are concerned about jellyfish when getting in the ocean – 2% more than those who are concerned about sharks.

Five percent of people who go to the beach do not get anywhere near the ocean.

Most important qualities of a beach

1	Cleanliness	⁸........%
2	View	46%
3	⁹........................	34%
4	Water temperature	23%

And the most popular beach in the nation is …

Waikiki in ¹⁰........................

LISTENING TIP

Filling in blanks to complete a text

- Read the directions carefully, so you know what the topic is going to be.
- Find the blanks and look carefully at the words before and after them. Then guess what kind of information you will be listening for. For example, is it a number or the name of a country?

- Listen carefully for numbers. If you are unsure, write the number which makes the most sense.
- Finally, it might sound obvious, but if the question asks you to fill in the blank with one word, then only use one word – not more.

Unit check

1 Fill in the blanks

Complete the text with the words in the box.

> beaches ~~Islands~~ for off ocean
> on in reefs journey ever

Lying just off the coast of Lombok, the Gili _____Islands_____ must be the most beautiful place I've
[1] _____ seen. These three tiny islands were like jewels sparkling in the middle of the [2] _____ .
Beautiful sandy [3] _____ , clear blue ocean and wonderful coral [4] _____ were nearby for
snorkeling. We went [5] _____ vacation there last year and had a great time. Getting there was quite
a [6] _____ , though. We left [7] _____ Indonesia from Los Angeles late on a Sunday evening and
arrived Monday afternoon in Bali in the middle of a huge thunderstorm. We got [8] _____ the plane
and then we got [9] _____ a taxi to Lombok. This also involved getting on a ferry. Then we got on
a boat to the Gili Islands. After 40 hours of traveling, we finally arrived.

[9]

2 Choose the correct answers

Circle the correct answer: a, b or c.

1 They've gone _____ for a few days.
  a in   b out   c (away)

2 Our clothes have _____ before the trip.
  a to be washed   b to wash   c washed

3 Do the reservations _____ in advance?
  a need to make   b need to be made
  c needed to make

4 The _____ was surrounded by nothing but water.
  a bay   b island   c lake

5 _____ on the beach, life couldn't get any better.
  a Read   b Reading   c To read

6 We were in the middle of a _____ , nothing but sand for miles around.
  a desert   b glacier   c bay

7 We arrived late because we set _____ later than we had planned.
  a for   b on   c off

8 I _____ the early train.
  a didn't need to be taken   b didn't need to take
  c needed to be taken

9 We're going to _____ for Canada tomorrow.
  a go   b leave   c take

[8]

3 Vocabulary

Underline the correct words.

1 I'm just going on / _for_ / off a quick walk. I'll be back soon.

2 My daughter's going _backpacking_ / _backhiking_ / _backcamping_ in South America for six months.

3 I'm not sure what time we'll get _over_ / _down_ / _back_, so don't wait up for us.

4 There were thousands of tiny fish swimming around the coral _reef_ / _plain_ / _glacier_.

5 It's a really long trip, so I think we'll have a _layover_ / _voyage_ / _cruise_ somewhere.

6 They went fishing at the _desert_ / _lake_ / _canyon_.

7 It will be the first manned _voyage_ / _tour_ / _cruise_ to the moon in ten years.

8 We looked down from the top of the _bay_ / _cliff_ / _canyon_ at the waves below us.

9 The band will be _for_ / _in_ / _on_ tour until next April.

[8]

How did you do?

Total: [25]

| Very good 25 – 20 | OK 19 – 16 | Review Unit 14 again 15 or less |

15 Natural health

1 Grammar

* Passive report structures

a Read the text and <u>underline</u> five more examples of passive report structures.

How dolphins communicate

Bottle-nosed dolphins <u>are known to be</u> the most intelligent mammals after humans. One of the reasons for this is because of their amazing ability to "speak" with each other. A large part of their brain is believed to be used for a communication system, which is very well developed in dolphins.

Although experts are not 100% sure, dolphins are also thought to have their own formal language. Each dolphin is believed to have its own whistle, almost as if it was its name.

Dolphins can't produce sounds in the same way as humans. They don't have vocal cords at the back of their throat like we do.

Instead they use a complicated system of sounds, such as whistles, squeaks, moans and clicks, produced by the muscles in the blowhole, a small hole on the top of the dolphins' heads. This sound system is known to be particularly useful at night or in dark waters as it also allows the dolphin to find its way even if it can't see very well. Dolphins are known to be able to produce sound frequencies from 0.25 to 200 kHz, with the lower frequencies used for communication.

b Read the newspaper extracts. Do the <u>underlined</u> parts of each sentence refer to the past or the present? Write *past* or *present*.

1 The million dollar lottery winner is believed <u>to live</u> in the Boston area. *present*

2 More than 50 people are believed <u>to have been killed</u> by the storm. ....

3 The thieves are thought <u>to have entered</u> the museum last weekend. ....

4 The president is said <u>to have been</u> very happy about the news. ....

5 The man is known <u>to be</u> dangerous.

    ....

6 The movie, which is believed <u>to have cost</u> more than $100 million, opens on Friday.

    ....

c Rewrite the following sentences using passive report structures.

1 Scientists think dinosaurs were wiped out by an ice age.

    Dinosaurs are thought to have been wiped out by an ice age.

2 People say this plant is good at helping you relax.

    This plant ....

    ....

3 Scientists think that elephants have good memories.

    Elephants ....

    ....

4 Experts believe this plant was used by our ancestors to cure headaches.

    This plant ....

    ....

5 Scientists say the last part of the forest was cut down more than 100 years ago.

    The last part of the forest ....

    ....

6 People know that some modern medicines actually do us harm.

    Some modern medicines ....

    ....

2 Vocabulary

✳ Health and medicine

a Find four words or phrases to do with health and medicine in the wordsnake.

emergencyroomanestheticsurgeondiagnosis

1 _____ 2 _____ 3 _____ 4 _____

b Complete the dialogue with the words in the box.

symptoms   recovering   ~~doctor~~   diet   get better   check-up   suffer   diagnosed

Woman: Hello, you must be the new ___doctor___ .

Doctor: Yes, I'm Dr. Lane. Are you here for a
¹ _____ ?

Woman: No, I haven't been feeling well recently.

Doctor: What are your ² _____ ?

Woman: I often ³ _____ from headaches, and
I'm ⁴ _____ from the flu right now.

Doctor: Have you ever been ⁵ _____ with any
serious illnesses?

Woman: No.

Doctor: Let me see. I think you may need some vitamins.

Woman: Will I need to change my ⁶ _____ ?

Doctor: No, just take this medication, and you should
⁷ _____ soon.

3 Pronunciation

✳ /n/ thi_n_ and /ŋ/ thi_ng_

a ▶ **CD4 T31** Listen and (circle) the word you hear.

1 Some drugs are used in hospitals to (thin)/ thing your blood.

2 Janet is in the recovery win / wing in the hospital.

3 The government can ban / bang medicine that is harmful.

4 Do you think Dr. Stevens will win / wing a Best Doctor of America award?

5 Did you hear that loud ban / bang?

6 Frank broke his leg after he ran / rang and fell.

7 Sheila hurt her fingers on the run / rung of a ladder.

8 What type of thin / thing did the doctor diagnose?

b ▶ **CD4 T31** Listen and repeat.

4 Vocabulary

⭐ Feelings

a ▶ **CD4 T32** Listen to the conversation and match the two parts of the sentences. Write a–f on the lines.

1	Katie's feeling sorry for herself	*e*	a	and it's making him exhausted.
2	Dan's over-anxious about his school work,	....	b	and it makes her panicky.
3	Nick feels guilty	....	c	and it's getting her down.
4	Julia doesn't have any confidence in herself	....	d	when he gets jealous.
5	Grandma's very nostalgic,	....	e	because she's homesick.
6	Abby is absent-minded,	....	f	and she always talks about when she was young.

b Read the text about emotional well-being. Some lines are correct and some have a word which should not be there. If a line is correct, put a check (✓) in the blank at the end of the line. If a word should not be there, cross it out and write the word in the blank.

If you are feeling i̶t̶ anxious or depressed you may consider	1	*it*
keeping a thought journal. The first thing you should do is	2	✓
think about your problem and decide what can it is that is	3	....
making you panicky or depressed. It's not important to figure on	4	....
out what that the cause is at this stage. The next step is to	5	....
rate how very bad the problem is and pay attention to when it	6	....
occurs. You may notice that a pattern. Now you need to	7	....
decide what action you need to take and what behaviors you	8	....
should to change first. Don't lose your confidence at this	9	....
stage. It's easy to feel sorry for yourself and to think you'll	10	....
never manage to change. Once you have decided on to your goals	11	....
you need to work toward them at in your own time. Don't feel	12	....
guilty if you are not going as fast as you hoped you would.	13	....

c **Vocabulary bank** Replace the underlined words with a word or phrase from the box.

> on top of the world   j̶e̶a̶l̶o̶u̶s̶   down   uneasy   over the moon   in a good mood   irritable   uptight

1 My older brother thinks that Mom and Dad spoil me.
He gets so <u>unhappy because I have what he wants</u>. *jealous*

2 I didn't do very well on the test, so I'm a little <u>depressed</u> right now. ....

3 I don't think he really likes little children much, so I'm always a little
<u>worried and uncomfortable</u> when I take the kids to see him. ....

4 That's great news. I'm <u>very pleased</u> for you. ....

5 Don't get <u>worried and nervous</u> . It's only a soccer game. It's
not the end of the world. ....

6 She said "Yes." She's going to marry me! I'm <u>extremely happy</u>. ....

7 Kevin is always <u>happy</u>, but his brother rarely is. ....

8 Don't talk to Dad today. He's very <u>easily annoyed</u>. ....

Culture in mind

a Read the text quickly and find the names of seven diseases.

Sanitation

A few years ago *The British Medical Journal* launched a competition to decide the greatest medical breakthrough of all time. Fifteen "discoveries" were submitted, and the case for each was argued by prominent doctors from around the world. The shortlist included breakthroughs such as vaccines, the dangers of smoking, DNA and the use of computers. Members of the public were then invited to vote for which one they felt was the most important. After more than 11,000 people had sent in their choices, the winner was finally announced. And with 1,975 votes the winner was ... sanitation.

Sanitation, which includes all aspects of delivering clean water to homes and taking the dirty water away, was championed by Professor Johan Mackenbach from the University Medical Center, Rotterdam, for the following reasons:

The Industrial Revolution was a time of great change. Before then, most people lived in the countryside and worked on the land. But the Industrial Revolution saw the opening of huge factories, which led to the mass movement of people from rural living to towns. It also brought with it the need for sanitation.

At first, the connection between crowded living conditions and illness went unrecognized, and infectious diseases were responsible for a great number of deaths. Tuberculosis, dysentery, diphtheria, typhoid, measles and smallpox were all common killers.

It was the cholera epidemic of the mid 19th century which started people thinking. John Snow, involved in the development of anesthesia, was the one to show that shutting off a particular pump, in London's Broad Street, stopped the spread of cholera in the area.

But it was Edwin Chadwick, a lawyer, who came up with the idea of sewers and piped drinking water linked to people's houses to cut the risk of infection from poor urban drainage.

It took decades for his idea to be accepted. But it was, and between 1901 and 1970, deaths from diarrhea and dysentery fell by around 12% in the UK.

In the 21st century, good sanitation is still a major problem in the developing world. Unsafe water, sanitation and hygiene were estimated to account for around 88% of the 1.8 million deaths from diarrheal disease in low and middle-income countries in 2001.

b Read the text again and answer the questions.

1 How was the winner of *The British Medical Journal*'s competition decided?

2 What is sanitation?

3 How did the Industrial Revolution change life in the UK?

4 How did crowded living conditions cause a rise in killer diseases?

5 What was John Snow's contribution to sanitation?

6 What was Edwin Chadwick's idea?

7 What were the results of a good sanitation system in the UK?

8 What evidence is there that poor sanitation remains a problem in much of the world?

Skills in mind

6 Read and write

Complete the dialogue with the correct
words a, b, c or d.

COMPUTER
LAB

Paula: Hi Joe, ¹ _____how come_____ you're so early?

Joe: I'm nervous ² _____ the
computer exam.

Paula: Don't worry, you'll be fine.

Joe: No, I'm just ³ _____ the
money for the exam. I'm not ready for it yet.

Paula: Don't say that, Joe. You're giving up
before you try.

Joe: I can't see myself passing.

Paula: Well, Joe, if you want to pass, you need
to change that. You need to see yourself
passing.

Joe: ⁴ _____ than done.

Paula: ⁵ _____ a minute and listen
to me!

Joe: OK, go ahead.

Paula: If you see yourself failing, you'll fail. If you
see yourself passing, you'll pass.

Joe: I might as well try. I'll try ⁶ _____
at this stage.

Paula: If you think positively, you're
⁷ _____ to success!

1	a how long	b (how come)	c come on	d sort of
2	a of	b with	c about	d at
3	a throwing away	b throwing out	c throwing up	d throwing in
4	a Easy to	b Easier	c Better to say	d Easier said
5	a Hang in	b Hang out	c Hang up	d Hang on
6	a everything	b anything	c something	d nothing
7	a well on	b well done	c well on your way	d well down the way

EXAM TIP

Multiple-choice cloze

- Read the text all the way through before you
  try to complete the sentences.

- Then read each sentence very carefully and
  try to understand what it will mean when the
  blank is filled.

- When you think you have found the correct
  answer, check that both the grammar and
  meaning are correct. If you are unsure, try
  saying the sentence to yourself with the
  other options in the blank. Do any of them
  sound right?

- Remember, you should always write
  something, even if you really don't know the
  answer. A sensible guess is usually better than
  no answer at all.

7 Study help

✶ Learning new words

When you learn new words and
phrases in English, notice word
combinations. Notice the difference
between expressions such as *You're
well* and *You're well on your way*. It's
important to understand how words
are used, not just their individual
meanings. When you are reading
a text, underline or highlight any
unexpected or unusual combinations
of words. See if you can figure out
the meaning from the context, and
then check it in a dictionary. Try to
understand the meaning by making
sentences that are meaningful to
you using that particular word
combination.

Unit check

1 Fill in the blanks

Complete the text with the words in the box.

> symptoms   is believed   felt   taking   medical
> doctor   specialized   ~~diagnosed~~   medicine
> was performing

Jonathan was __*diagnosed*__ with a rare skin problem. He was prescribed a strong medicine by a
¹ _____ , but his condition gradually got worse.

Then one evening he went to see a hypnotist who ² _____ at the town hall. Jonathan was
hypnotized in front of an audience. The next day he felt much better. He even forgot to take his medicine,
but he ³ _____ fine. Jonathan told his doctor, who told him to see a ⁴ _____
hypnotist who ⁵ _____ in Jonathan's problem. That was three years ago. Jonathan has stopped
⁶ _____ most of his medicine and his ⁷ _____ have disappeared. Hypnotism
⁸ _____ to be a powerful ⁹ _____ by many doctors.

| | 9 |

2 Choose the correct answers

Circle the correct answer: a, b or c.

1 Her car _____ in last week's crash.
   a is destroyed   b destroyed   c (was destroyed)

2 The new computer store _____ to be excellent.
   a says   b is said   c saying

3 Children are often _____ to be faster language learners than adults.
   a said   b saying   c have said

4 She had her temperature _____ by the nurse.
   a taken   b done   c made

5 When was your last _____ at the doctor's?
   a check-up   b check-in   c check out

6 I _____ from car sickness since I was a child.
   a was suffering   b have suffered   c am suffering

7 He's known to _____ of cholera.
   a be dead   b dead   c have died

8 Five percent of the population are _____ with depression every year.
   a suffered   b operated   c diagnosed

9 It is _____ by some scientists that certain plants can heal illnesses.
   a thought   b have thought   c thinking | 8 |

3 Vocabulary

Rewrite the sentences using the word in parentheses.

1 He tends to get very worried, very quickly. (panicky)
   He's very panicky. _____

2 We were so happy when we heard the news. (moon)
   _____

3 I couldn't be happier. (world)
   _____

4 Don't worry so much. (anxious)
   _____

5 He got better really quickly. (recovery)
   _____

6 She had a really bad headache. (suffering)
   _____

7 He forgets everything I tell him. (minded)
   _____

8 The doctor wants to cut the tumor out. (operate)
   _____

9 I went to the doctor to make sure everything is OK. (check-up)
   _____

| | 8 |

How did you do?

Total: | 25 |

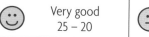 Very good
25 – 20

 OK
19 – 16

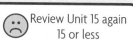 Review Unit 15 again
15 or less

16 Movie magic

1 Grammar

✳ Infinitive of purpose: *to / in order to / so as to*

a Match the two parts of the sentences.

1 I got up at 5:00 a.m. in order to — _b_
2 Dad took the car to the mechanic to — ....
3 The charity gave them an extra week so as to — ....
4 The government kept it a secret in order not to — ....
5 Mom told us to turn the music down in order not to — ....
6 We booked a hotel online so as not to — ....

a give them more time to raise the money for the medical supplies.
b take some photos of the sunrise.
c create a public panic.
d waste time looking for one when we got there.
e get the brakes checked.
f wake up Dad.

b Choose the correct words to complete the story.

X-Men IV was going to be the biggest movie of the year. I had to be at the movie theater on the day that it opened ¹ (*so as not to*) */ so as to* lose my status of being the world's biggest X-Men fan.

I bought my ticket two weeks before on the Internet ² *so as not to / so as to* make sure I'd get one. I didn't want to arrive at the theater and find they'd sold out.

I left home at 1:00 p.m. ³ *in order not to / in order to* arrive at the theater early and avoid the line. At the movie theater, I stopped at the candy counter ⁴ *not to / to* buy snacks and a soda. I bought a lot ⁵ *so as not to / so as to* have to leave the movie in the middle if I got hungry.

I got a seat right at the front ⁶ *in order not to / in order to* run the risk of a big, tall man sitting in front of me and blocking the screen. I turned off my cell phone ⁷ *in order not to / in order to* be disturbed and because a big ad on the screen told me to. Then the movie started, and I sat back in my seat ⁸ *not to / to* enjoy the movie. It was only then that I realized I'd left my glasses at home.

c Join the two sentences to make one. Use the word in **bold** at the end.

1 I got up at 6:00 a.m. I wanted to drive my friend to the airport. **(to)**
   I got up at 6:00 a.m. to drive my friend to the airport.

2 We got to the stadium early. We didn't want to miss the start of the game. **(in order not to)**
   ....
   ....

3 I called Michelle. I wanted to invite her to my party. **(so as to)**
   ....
   ....

4 I didn't tell Ahmed about the accident. I didn't want to worry him. **(so as not to)**
   ....
   ....

5 I took the train. I didn't want to get caught in a traffic jam. **(in order not to)**
   ....
   ....

6 I'd like to speak to her. I want to apologize. **(so as to)**
   ....
   ....

7 He's saving all his money. He wants to buy a new computer. **(to)**
   ....
   ....

8 Can you speak quietly? You are disturbing other people. **(so as not to)**
   ....
   ....

2 Grammar

✱ Result clauses with *so / such (that)*

a Underline the correct option.

1 We've lived here *so* / *such* long that we don't even notice the planes anymore.

2 It was *so* / *such* an easy test that everyone passed.

3 It was *so* / *such* dark that we couldn't see a thing.

4 I've eaten *so* / *such* much food I could explode.

5 He was *so* / *such* tired that he just wanted to go to bed.

6 It was *so* / *such* a long movie that most people fell asleep before the end.

b Complete the sentences with *so* or *such*.

1 I have ___such___ a bad memory that things just slip my mind all the time.

2 I'm _____ scared of pain that I always ask the dentist to give me a painkiller.

3 She spends _____ much time on the phone that I never get a chance to use it.

4 Dave's _____ a funny guy that I can't help laughing whenever I'm with him.

5 She went to _____ great lengths to arrange this party for you. You should at least say "thank you."

6 They've had _____ a bad falling out that I don't think they'll make up this time.

7 We have _____ many signatures on our petition that they'll have to pay attention to us.

8 I'm _____ tired that I can't stop yawning.

c Join the two sentences to make one. Use *so / such ... that*.

1 I'm really tired. I'm going to bed early tonight.

I'm so tired that I'm going to bed early tonight.

2 Nick is really careless. He breaks something every time he comes to my house.

----

3 We left very late. We didn't arrive until midnight.

----

4 That's a nasty cough. You should see a doctor.

----

5 Our team played badly. We were beaten 5–1.

----

6 Rob's a really intellectual person. It's difficult to understand everything he talks about.

----

7 The walk-a-thon was a great success. We're going to organize another one.

----

8 He snored really loudly. I couldn't get to sleep.

----

3 Pronunciation

✱ Word stress in multisyllabic words

a ▶ CD4 T33 Listen and mark the stress on each word.

1 million
2 millionaire
3 confront
4 confrontation
5 problem
6 problematic
7 adapt
8 adaptation
9 recommend
10 recommendation

b ▶ CD4 T33 Listen again and repeat.

4 Vocabulary

★ Reacting to movies

a Read the sentences and write the numbers 1–8 in the correct boxes.

1 Jessica jumped out of her seat.
2 Frank fell over laughing.
3 Yoshi couldn't stop yawning.
4 Charlie chuckled.
5 Carol cried her eyes out.
6 Erika was on the edge of her seat.
7 Sara screamed.
8 Brian bit his lip.

b What real movies do you think each of these people might be watching? Give your reasons.

1 Jessica might be watching _Scream III because it's a very scary movie._
2 Frank might be watching _____.
3 Yoshi might be watching _____.
4 Charlie might be watching _____.
5 Carol might be watching _____.
6 Erika might be watching _____.
7 Sara might be watching _____.
8 Brian might be watching _____.

c Complete the sentences with the words in the box.

> laughing   crying   sitting   screaming   jumping   chuckling   ~~yawning~~   biting

1 I was so tired that I couldn't stop __yawning__ .
2 Why are you _____ to yourself? What's so funny?
3 You could hardly hear the band play because there were so many teenage girls _____ .
4 We spent the whole game _____ on the edge of our seats. It was so exciting.
5 It was so funny we fell over _____ .
6 I spent the whole movie _____ my lip. I was determined not to cry.
7 My mom spent the whole wedding _____ her eyes out.
8 The movie had us _____ out of our seats every five minutes.

d **Vocabulary bank** Complete the sentences with the words in the box.

> tremble   nails   face   laugh   joy   hands   hair   ~~goosebumps~~

1 I get _goosebumps_ just thinking about talking to her.
2 I know you're nervous but try not to bite your _____ .
3 He won't listen to anything I say. He makes me want to pull my _____ out.
4 Mom cried for _____ when I told her I passed my driving test.
5 When my dad asked Tom if he was my boyfriend, I just hid my _____ in my hands.
6 The movie was so funny it made me _____ out loud.
7 Dad threw his _____ up in horror when I told him I'd crashed his car.
8 As I sat there waiting for the exam to begin, I started to _____ .

5 Everyday English

a Put the words in order to make expressions.

a   the / to / it's / me / same / all   _It's all the same to me._

b   the / tongue / of / tip / it's / on / my   ....

c   rings / that / bell / a   ....

d   and / that / this   ....

e   mind / in / have / anything   ....

f   way / the / through / all   ....

b Read the dialogue. Replace the <u>underlined</u> phrases with the expressions in Exercise 5a. Write a–f in the boxes.

Ana: Hey, Paula. What do you have planned this weekend?

Paula: [1]<u>A few different things</u>. Nothing special, though. Why? ☐

Ana: Do you want to do something this evening?

Paula: Sure. Why not? [2]<u>Have you already made any plans</u>? ☐

Ana: Not really. [3]<u>I don't care what we do</u>. What about you? ☐

Paula: Well, I wouldn't mind going to the movies.

Ana: That's a great idea. What's playing?

Paula: There's that new movie with ... oh, what's his name? [4]<u>I can't quite remember it</u>. You know... ☐

Ana: No, I don't. Who?

Paula: That one who was in all those movies about kids singing at school.

Ana: Do you mean _High School Musical_?

Paula: [5]<u>That sounds familiar</u>. Yeah. That's the movie. Who was in that? ☐

Ana: Only my favorite actor, Zac Efron.

Paula: Yeah. That's him. I wouldn't mind seeing his new movie.

Ana: I've already seen it five times.

Paula: So I don't suppose you'd want to watch it [6]<u>from the beginning to the end</u> again? ☐

Ana: Of course I would! I love him.

6 Study help

 ✱ Checking your writing

It's not always easy to spot the mistakes in your own writing. Ideally, you should get someone else to look at your work and help you if you can. If this isn't possible, try to follow these guidelines:

● As soon as you finish, quickly read your work and correct any obvious mistakes you see. Do not try to do a complete check now. Often you will only see exactly what you think you have written.

● Wait for a while (a day or two if you have time) and return to your writing with fresh eyes. Read through your work at a normal speed. This is just to remind you of what you have written and for you to get an overall impression of your work. Do not correct anything at this stage.

● Now read it again more carefully. Take each sentence one at a time and read it to yourself slowly. Read exactly what you see on the page – not what you think should be there. Make corrections.

● Read your work one last time. It's a good idea to do this out loud if possible, because then you can hear if it sounds natural and reads easily.

● If you have any questions about the organization of the writing, or the grammar or vocabulary, ask your teacher if you can write these questions at the bottom of your writing. Then your teacher can answer them.

Now your writing should be ready to hand in.

7 Read

a Read the DVD recommendations and, for each one, <u>underline</u> the names of the director and the leading actors.

b Read the texts again. Put phrases 1–6 into the correct places.

1 to stop being part of the show
2 has no idea about how he is being exploited
3 to save a failing TV station
4 to stay in the real world forever
5 to take a break from everyday life
6 to be seen by millions of viewers

DVD Decisions – Looking for a good movie to rent? Let us help you.

Fiction or Reality?

Here are some recommendations for classic movies to watch this weekend – each of them explores the themes of cinema, fiction and reality.

The Purple Rose of Cairo (1985)

One reason to go to the movies is
A _____ and lose yourself in the magic of the silver screen. In *The Purple Rose of Cairo*, Woody Allen turns this idea on its head.

Mia Farrow plays Cecilia, a New Jersey waitress, who goes to the local movie theater to escape from her boring life. Jeff Daniels is Tom Baxter, the handsome archaeologist hero in a movie called *The Purple Rose of Cairo*, which Cecilia has already seen several times. One day, Baxter decides he's had enough of being a character in a movie, and he walks out of the screen to join Cecilia in the theater. Can Hollywood find Tom and get him back into the movie or will he manage B _____ ?

EDtv (1999)

A television studio executive (Ellen DeGeneres) has an idea about how E _____ – film and broadcast a normal person's life 24 hours a day. *EDtv* is born the moment her eye falls on Ed Pekurny, a friendly video store clerk played by Matthew McConaughey. After the show's first week on air, Ed's fame grows and grows, but then conflicts start up, particularly with Ed's girlfriend and his family. After a while, Ed decides he wants F _____ , but he finds out his contract can't be reversed. But in a country that switches the TV set on at breakfast and off at bedtime, anything can happen... Ron Howard's comedy is well worth watching.

The Truman Show (1998)

As a movie fan, do you also enjoy TV reality shows?

In reality shows, people choose
C _____ – but what if they didn't even know they were in a show? Peter Weir's *The Truman Show* takes this idea and plays with it wonderfully.

Jim Carrey is Truman, a man whose life is fake. His hometown is really a huge studio with hidden cameras everywhere, and all his friends and the people around him (even his wife, played by Laura Linney) are actors in the most popular TV series in the world: *The Truman Show*, directed by Christof (the actor Ed Harris), the man who actually runs Truman's life. Truman believes he is an ordinary man with an ordinary life, and D _____ – until one day, when he finds out everything. His attempt to break away and start his own, unwatched life is moving and thought-provoking.

Unit check

1 Fill in the blanks

Complete the text with the words in the box.

> such   chuckled   order   should   not
> a   so   ~~comedy~~   end   over

The last movie I saw was a __comedy__ called *The Pink Panther*. It's about a detective named Inspector Clouseau. He is called in by the French police in ¹_____ to solve a diamond robbery. The only problem is that Clouseau has ²_____ many accidents that whatever he does always ends in disaster. It stars Steve Martin, who is such ³_____ good actor that I fell ⁴_____ laughing every time he was in a scene. It was ⁵_____ a funny movie! I won't say any more so as ⁶_____ to give the ⁷_____ of the movie away, which is terrific, by the way. I went with my dad. He only ⁸_____ to himself a few times. He told me that I ⁹_____ see the original movie from the 1960s with an actor named Peter Sellers.

| 9 |

2 Choose the correct answers

Circle the correct answer: a, b or c.

1 I didn't want to cry so I bit my _____ .
   a mouth   b cheek   c (lip)

2 I spoke to the manager _____ complain.
   a for to   b so as   c in order to

3 It was _____ a hot day that I felt sick.
   a so   b such   c really

4 The game was so exciting that we were on the _____ of our seats for ninety minutes.
   a side   b top   c edge

5 I called him _____ invite him to my party.
   a to   b for   c so

6 He must have said something funny because everyone fell _____ laughing.
   a about   b over   c out

7 We're _____ happy that we're going out tonight to celebrate.
   a too   b so   c such

8 The movie was so sad that I cried my eyes _____ .
   a over   b out   c up

9 We set off really early _____ as not to get stuck in traffic.
   a for   b to   c so

| 8 |

3 Vocabulary

What are the words? Complete the sentences.

1 When he told us what happened, we all just lefl ___fell___ over laughing.
2 I was so scared that I started giitbn _____ my lip.
3 It's so cold that I have sogoepubms _____ .
4 The book wasn't hilarious, but I did find myself lucihkncg _____ a few times.
5 If you can't stop wanngiy _____ , you should go to bed.
6 She threw her hands up in rrroho _____ when she saw the mess we had made in the living room.
7 When the monster made its first appearance, I pejmud _____ out of my seat.
8 I know it's a bad habit, but I can't help biting my slain _____ , especially when I'm nervous.
9 When the actors got out of the limousine, all their fans started grimacens _____ .

| 8 |

How did you do?

Total: | 25 |

| :) | Very good 25 – 20 | :\| | OK 19 – 16 | :(| Review Unit 16 again 15 or less |

Vocabulary bank

Unit 4 Personality

1   **calm** = quiet and relaxed
    Helen never seems to get angry or excited.
    She's a very **calm** person.

2   **excitable** = easily and
    often excited
    He's a nice boy,
    but he's very
    excitable when
    he's with other
    children.

3   **smart** = intelligent
    My sister got 95% on her
    tests at school. She's very **smart**!

4   **eccentric** = acting in a
    strange or unusual
    way – sometimes
    an amusing way
    My uncle Joe is a
    little **eccentric**.
    He only ever
    wears a suit and tie,
    even at home!

5   **upbeat** = full of positive feelings
    He's always happy and smiling. He's a really
    upbeat person.

6   **(in)considerate** = (not)
    thinking about
    other people's
    feelings and
    interests
    Our neighbors
    are playing
    music loudly
    again. They're so
    inconsiderate!

7   **(un)selfish** = (not) thinking only about your
    own advantage
    He could have scored the goal himself, but
    he was **unselfish** and passed the ball for
    another player to score.

8   **(un)approachable** = (not) friendly and easy
    to talk to
    If you have a problem, go and talk
    to our teacher – you know, he's very
    approachable.

Unit 5 Expressions with "time"

1   **time's up** = the time allowed (e.g., for an examination, or
    in a sports game) has finished
    "OK, everyone – **time's up**, so please stop writing and
    hand in your answer papers."

2   **at all times** = always
    "Please keep your luggage with you **at all times**. Luggage
    left unattended will be taken away."

3   **no time to lose** = something must be done immediately
    "The game starts in ten minutes and we <u>must</u> watch it!
    Come on, there's **no time to lose**!"

4   **of all time** = that has ever lived or existed
    Many people think that Roger Federer is the greatest
    tennis player **of all time**.

5   **from time to time** = occasionally, sometimes
    I don't particularly like sweet things, but I eat a piece of
    chocolate **from time to time**.

6   **time to kill** = a period of time when you have nothing
    to do
    "We have some **time to kill** before our train leaves.
    Should we go have some coffee?"

7   **at the time** = at the particular point when something
    was thought or done.
    "Buying this laptop was a big mistake, but I thought it
    was a good idea **at the time**."

8   **a matter of time** = used when you think something will
    happen in the near future
    "I've been late for school three times this week. It's only
    a matter of time before the teacher loses his patience
    with me."

9   **to have time** (for something) = to be available to do
    something
    "Do you **have time** to help me with my homework?"

10 **to have the time of (your) life** = a very enjoyable
    experience
    "Your party was fantastic! I **had the time of my life**."

Unit 6 Adverbial phrases

1 backward

I got dressed in a hurry this morning, and I put my sweater on **backward**.

2 from head to toe

The car drove through the puddle and splashed water all over me. I got wet **from head to toe**.

3 inside out (1)

"I'm going to show you around the castle, and you can ask me any questions you want. I know this place **inside out**."

4 inside out (2)

"Hey, Alex – I can see the label of your T-shirt. I think you have it on **inside out**."

5 from top to bottom

The kitchen was filthy, so on Sunday we cleaned it **from top to bottom**.

6 upside down (1)

"I turned my bedroom **upside down**, but I still couldn't find my passport!"

7 upside down (2)

The display was wonderful. At one point, the planes were flying **upside down**!

8 the wrong way

"Well, of course it doesn't work. You put the batteries in **the wrong way**."

Unit 7 Ways of getting involved

1 to give someone a hand = to help someone
"I'm having a lot of problems with my homework. Can you **give me a hand**, Mom?"

2 to volunteer = to do something freely that you don't have to do
My brother didn't have to join the army, but he **volunteered**, and now he's a soldier.

3 with the aid of = with help or support
My grandma's very old, but she can still walk **with the aid of** a cane.

4 in aid of = in order to help
We're collecting money **in aid of** poor children in Africa.

5 aid worker = someone who is working in a country where there is a war, no food, etc., in order to help people
Before she started work as a doctor, Sara was an **aid worker** in Africa.

6 to collaborate = to work together with another person or other people
The firefighters and the police **collaborated** to make sure the building was safe.

7 to back = to give help/support with money or with words
The government has decided **to back** plans for research, and will give $5 million.

Unit 9 Conflicts and solutions

1   **to not be on speaking terms (with someone)** = to refuse to speak to someone because you are angry with them
    They had an argument last night, and now they're **not on speaking terms** (with each other).

2   **a quarrel** = an argument or disagreement
    They had **a quarrel** about three months ago, and they haven't spoken to each other since.

3   **to pick a fight with someone** = to start a fight with someone
    He was in a really bad mood, so he just **picked a fight** with the first person he saw.

4   **to come to blows** = to have a physical fight with someone
    They argued and shouted for ages, but fortunately, they didn't **come to blows**.

5   **to negotiate** = to talk together to try to reach an agreement
    The teachers and the school board **are negotiating** salary and vacation time.

6   **a misunderstanding** = a small disagreement
    We argued a little last night. Well, it wasn't really an argument, just a **misunderstanding**.

7   **ill feeling** = an unpleasant feeling between people who do not like each other
    He accused me of stealing from him! So there's a lot of **ill feeling** between us now.

8   **give-and-take** = the willingness to discuss things with people so that you can live together easily
    In every friendship there has to be some **give-and-take**.

9   **to get to the bottom of (something)** = to discover the facts/truth about a situation
    I don't know what caused the problem, but I'm working **to get to the bottom of** it.

10 **to take the bull by the horns** = to do something difficult in a brave, determined way
    I really wanted to know the answer, so I **took the bull by the horns** and wrote an email to the president!

Unit 10 Making an effort

1   **to make an/no attempt** = to (not) try to do something, especially something difficult
    I tried to talk to him, but he **made no attempt** to be friendly, so I left.

2   **to (not) bother** = to (not) make the effort to do something
    He could have called me, but he just didn't **bother**.

3   **can't be bothered** = to be too lazy or uninterested to do something
    I know I should read this book for my project, but I **can't be bothered**, so I'm going to watch TV.

4   **to sweat (over something)** = to work very hard
    I've been **sweating over** this math problem for an hour, but I can't solve it!

5   **no sweat** [informal] = it isn't difficult / not a problem
    "Can you show me how to use this program on my laptop?"
    "Sure — **no sweat**."

6   **to be worth the effort** = to produce results which give value to the effort
    This food is really difficult to make — but it's so delicious, it's **worth the effort**.

7   **to put everything into (something)** = to work as hard as possible, make as much effort as possible
    He was only in fifth place, but then he **put everything into** the last 100 meters and he won!

8   **to make every effort** = to do your best to finish or accomplish something
    Thank you for your letter. We will **make every effort** to reply before the end of the week.

Unit 11 Language

1 **sign language** = the system of hand and body movements that deaf people use to communicate
My neighbor is deaf. It's amazing to watch her talking to her friends in **sign language**.

2 **slang** = very informal language, usually spoken rather than written
"Dough" is **slang** for "money" in the United States.

3 **an idiom** = a group of words in a fixed order that have a particular meaning, different from what the words on their own mean
To "bite off more than you can chew" is **an idiom** in English. It means to try to do something which is too difficult for you.

4 **a cliché** = an expression that is very often used, so it's not original or interesting
My wedding day – and I know it's **a cliché** – was just the happiest day of my life.

5 **to watch your language** = to be careful not to use rude or inappropriate language (often given as a warning)
There will be a lot of teachers at the party, so **watch your language**!

6 **a slogan** = a short and easily remembered phrase, especially one used to advertise an idea or a product
In his campaign to become president, Barack Obama used the **slogan** "Yes, we can"

7 **to (not) speak someone's language** = to (not) understand someone else's way of thinking or communicating
John and Meg are always talking about video games, and I can't understand what they're saying.
I just **don't speak their language**!

SIGN LANGUAGE

8 **to speak the same language** = to have similar ideas and similar ways of expressing them
We both come from New York and we both love baseball, so we **speak the same language**!

9 **terminology** = special words and phrases used by groups of people, especially in their work
It's hard to understand this letter from the lawyer because it's full of legal **terminology**.

10 **jargon** = the language used for a specific activity that is often not understood by people who don't do the activity
When Jim starts using computer **jargon**, I can't understand a word of what he's saying.

Unit 12 Expressions with "opinion"

1 **a matter of opinion** = something people can have different ideas about
Well, some people think it's a good idea, and some people don't – it's **a matter of opinion**.

2 **to express an opinion** = to say what you think about something
I don't know what he thinks about it. He didn't **express an opinion**.

3 **(my) humble opinion** = (my) modest opinion (to give an opinion without arrogance)
I'm no expert, but in **my humble opinion**, that's the wrong thing to do.

4 **a difference of opinion** = when people don't think the same way
We don't agree at all. Let's just say we have **a difference of opinion**.

5 **a second opinion** = another opinion, especially from a doctor
The doctor says my mom needs an operation, but we think she should get **a second opinion**.

6 **to have a high opinion of (yourself)** = to think (you) are skilled/smart, in a way that is annoying
Paul really makes me angry because he has such **a high opinion of himself**.

7 **an opinion poll** = when people are asked questions to discover what they think about a subject
The latest **opinion poll** shows that the president's popularity has gone down.

8 **public opinion** = what people in general think
The government wants to cut spending on education, but **public opinion** is against it.

Unit 13 Music

1 **an album** = a CD that has several pieces of music on it
Arcade Fire has a new CD out, and I think it's their best **album** so far.

2 **a track** = a song or piece of music on an album/CD
I like most of the songs on their new CD, but there are one or two pretty bad **tracks**, too.

3 **a soundtrack** = the music that is played during a movie
I didn't like the movie much, but there was some great music on **the soundtrack**.

4 **a (record) label** = a company that records and sells music
She's just signed a deal for four albums with a new **label**.

5 **elevator music** = music played in places like shopping malls
Everywhere you go in town, you hear **elevator music**, and it drives me crazy!

6 **a cover (version)** = a performance or recording of a song which was originally written and recorded by someone else
There have been millions of **covers** of Elvis Presley songs.

7 **a cover band** = a band or group that plays mostly, or only, cover songs
There's a **cover band** at the club tonight. They play music by the Beatles and the Rolling Stones.

8 **a composer** = a person who writes music
Mozart was one of the greatest **composers** of all time.

9 **a songwriter / singer-songwriter** = a person who writes / writes and sings songs
Who's your favorite **singer-songwriter**? Mine's Peter Gabriel.

Unit 14 Travel

1 **a journey** = the act of traveling from one place to another, especially in a car/bus/train/plane, etc.
We drove from New York to San Francisco. It was a long **journey** but we enjoyed it.

2 **a trip** = a journey in which you go somewhere, usually for a short time, and come back again
Last weekend we went on **a trip** to Paris.

3 **a voyage** = a long journey, especially by ship but also by, for example, spacecraft
Their **voyage** to the moon and back took eight days.

4 **a tour** = a journey made for pleasure, especially as a vacation, visiting several different places in an area
They've just come back from **a** walking **tour** of Boston.

5 **an excursion** = a short journey usually made for pleasure, often by a group of people
Our school went on **an excursion** to Quebec yesterday, but I didn't go.

6 **a cruise** = a journey for pleasure on a large ship, visiting several places
My mom's dream is to go on **a cruise** to the Caribbean Islands.

7 **backpacking** = traveling (usually cheaply) with your possessions in a backpack
When my daughter was 18, she went **backpacking** in South America.

8 **a layover** = a short stay that you make in a place while you are on a longer journey to somewhere else
We flew to South Korea last year, and we had a **layover** for two days in San Francisco.

9 **to commute** = to travel from your home to work and back, usually over a fairly long distance
He lives in New Jersey, but he **commutes** to New York City.

10 **an expedition** = an organized journey for a particular purpose
Dad and I are going on **a** shopping **expedition** to London tomorrow.

Unit 15 Feelings

1 **uptight** = worried or nervous, not able to relax
   Don't get **uptight** about the exam. It's not really that important.

2 **down** = unhappy, a little bit depressed
   I got some bad news today, so I'm feeling a little **down** right now.

3 **uneasy** = slightly worried or uncomfortable about a particular situation
   I want to ask her to help me, but I know she's very busy, so I feel a little **uneasy**.

4 **on top of the world** = very happy
   When I got the good news I was **on top of the world**.

5 **over the moon** = very happy
   I didn't think my team would win, so I was **over the moon** when they did!

6 **in a good mood** = very happy
   Look at her, smiling and singing. She's **in a good mood** today!

7 **envious** = wishing you had what another person has
   My friend Alex is going to Tahiti on vacation. I've always wanted to go there. I'm so **envious**!

8 **jealous** = unhappy or angry because someone might take something or someone that you love away from you
   I'm sure he likes my girlfriend. It makes me very **jealous**.

9 **irritable** = becoming angry or annoyed very easily
   Be careful what you say to him because he's very **irritable** today. He's shouted at me twice already!

Unit 16 Reactions

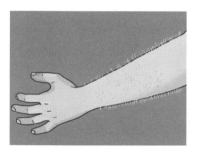

1 **to get goosebumps** [excitement, fear, anxiety]

2 **to cry for joy** [happiness]

3 **to throw your hands up in horror** [shock, horror]

4 **to bite your nails** [nervousness]

5 **to hide your face in your hands** [fear, embarrassment]

6 **to tremble** [fear]

7 **to pull your hair out** [frustration, anxiety]

8 **to laugh out loud** [amusement]

9 **to frown** [confusion, unhappiness]

Grammar reference

Unit 3

Relative clauses: review

1 We use relative clauses to add information about the subject or object of a sentence.

2 Relative clauses are introduced with words like *who, that, which, where* and *whose*.
We use *who* or *that* to refer to people.
*He's the man **who / that** wrote the article.*
We use *which* or *that* to refer to things.
*The newspaper **which / that** gives the best news is* The Daily Standard.
We use *where* to refer to places.
*That's the building **where** my sister works.*
We use *whose* to refer to possession.
*She's the woman **whose** house got destroyed in the flood.*

3 A defining relative clause gives essential information about the thing or person we are talking about. In this case we do not use a comma.
*The man **who** works in this office is very intelligent.*
(= I am talking about the only man who works in this office.)

4 A non-defining relative clause gives information that is additional about the thing or person we are talking about. The extra information is between commas.
The man, who works in this office, is very intelligent.
(= I am talking about an intelligent man and adding the non-essential information that he works in this office.)

Unit 4

what clauses

1 The word *what* can be used to mean *the thing that*, and can be used as the subject or object of a verb.
***What** (the thing that) makes me angry is the way he talks to people.* (subject)
*I can't remember **what** (the thing that) he said.* (object)

2 When *what* begins the sentence, we can use words like *that / why / when* (etc.) to join the second part of the sentence.
***What** you don't understand is **that** people are all different.*
***What** I don't like is **when** people want me to be the same as them.*

Verbs + gerund/infinitive review

Some verbs (*remember, stop, try*) can be followed by a second verb in either the gerund form or the infinitive form. The form of the second verb depends on the meaning of the sentence.

Remember
*I **remember calling** her to invite her. (= I called, and I remember that I did that.)*
*I **remembered to call** her and invite her. (= I almost forgot to call, but I remembered and then I called.)*

Stop
*The teacher **stopped talking** and left the room. (= The teacher was talking and then she stopped and left the room.)*
*When I was walking down the street, I **stopped to talk** to a friend of mine. (= I stopped walking, and after I stopped, I began to talk to a friend.)*

Try
*I **tried closing** the door but I could still hear the noise. (= It was noisy outside. I closed the door. When the door was closed, I could still hear the noise outside.)*
*I **tried to close** the door but it was stuck. (= I wanted to close the door, and I tried, but I was unsuccessful.)*

Unit 5

Reported speech review

1   When we report what someone said, there is often a change in verb tense between the direct speech (the person's actual words) and the indirect (reported) speech. The verb goes "one step back," e.g.

"I'm tired," he said yesterday.	→	*He said yesterday that he **was** tired.*
*"Someone **has stolen** my bicycle!" he said.*	→	*He said someone **had stolen** his bicycle.*
*"I **can't** lift this," she said.*	→	*She said that she **couldn't** lift it.*

We do not necessarily change the verb tense if the information in the direct speech is still true.

"He's Italian," she told me.	→	*She told me that he's Italian.*
*"I **was** born in Chicago," Amanda said.*	→	*Amanda said that she **was** born in Chicago.*

Reporting verbs review

We can use many different verbs to report speech. Note that the patterns that follow the verbs are different.

1   Some verbs (e.g., *say / state / emphasize*) are followed by *that* + clause.
   *He **emphasized that** the work was very important.*
   *The president **stated that** the economy had improved.*

2   Some verbs (e.g., *promise / refuse*) are followed by the infinitive with *to*.
   *She **promised to help** me in the evening.*
   *My father **refused to let** me stay out late.*
   Note that we can also use *promise* with the structure *promise* + person + *that*.
   *She **promised me that I could** take her to the movies.*

3   Some verbs (e.g., *encourage / advise / persuade*) are followed by an object (person) + the infinitive with *to*.
   *He **advised me to relax** more often.*
   *I **persuaded them to come** with me.*

4   Some verbs (e.g., *recommend / suggest / deny*) are followed by a noun or gerund.
   *I recommended **the new Coldplay CD / listening** to their new CD.*
   *They suggested **the French restaurant / eating** at the French restaurant.*

Unit 6

used to and *would*

1   We can use the expression *used to* + verb to talk about habits and customs in the past (things that are no longer true).
   *My father **used to drive**. (= My father drove in the past but he doesn't any more.)*
   *When I was young, I **used to go** swimming every day. (= That was my habit but I don't do this any more.)*

2   It is also possible to use *would* + verb to talk about habits and customs in the past.
   *My mother **would cook** chicken every Sunday. (= This was a custom of my mother's.)*
   *At school, I **would** always **ask** the teacher questions. (= This was a habit of mine when I was a child.)*

3   The difference between *used to* and *would* is that we can only use *would* for repeated actions, and we cannot use it for a permanent state or situation.
   *We **used to live** in Miami. (A permanent state or situation: We would live in Miami is not possible.)*
   *I used to visit my grandparents every weekend. (A repeated action: I **would visit** my grandparents every weekend is possible.)*

Adverbial phrases

1   We use adverbs to describe verbs — often, to say how an action is/was performed.
   *They played **well**.*
   *Drive more **slowly**!*
   *He reacted **angrily** to what I said.*

2   We can also use phrases to describe a verb and to say how an action is/was performed. These phrases are called **adverbial phrases** because they are like adverbs but are more than one word.

3   One structure for adverbial phrases is *with* + noun.
   *My brother looked at me **with surprise**.*
   *I finished my homework **with difficulty**.*
   *I listened to the show **with great interest**.*

4 Another structure for adverbial phrases is *in a(n)* + adjective + *way*.
*They asked me lots of questions, but **in a friendly way**.*
*We worked hard, but **in a fun way**.*
*I like listening to her because she talks **in an interesting way**.*

Adverbial phrases are often used when an adjective (e.g., *friendly, difficult, interesting, fun*) has no adverb form.

Unit 7

Conditionals review

1 We use the **zero conditional** to talk about a condition and consequence that are always true.
*If you **don't eat**, you **die**.*

2 We use the **first conditional** to talk about a possible present situation and its possible future consequence.
*If we **raise** enough money, we'll **build** a hospital.*

3 We use the **second conditional** to talk about a hypothetical situation in the present and its future consequence, which may be very unlikely or impossible.
*If I **were** president, I'd **increase** the money we spend on helping other countries.*

4 We use the **third conditional** to talk about a hypothetical situation and consequence in the past which is, therefore, impossible to change.
*If the food **had arrived** quicker, we'd **have** saved thousands of lives.*

Mixed conditionals

Conditional sentences do not always follow the four patterns described above. For example, it is common to find mixtures of second and third conditionals.

1 If we want to talk about a past action and its present consequence, then the *if* clause follows the pattern of a third conditional and the consequence clause follows the pattern of a second conditional.
*If more people **had signed** the petition, the shopping center **wouldn't be** here. (= Not many people signed the petition, so the shopping center is here.)*
*If I **hadn't missed** the plane, I'd **be** in Mexico now. (= I missed the plane. I'm not in Mexico.)*

2 If we want to talk about how a universal truth affected a past action, then the *if* clause follows the pattern of a second conditional and the consequence clause follows the pattern of a third conditional.
*If the world **were** a fairer place, those people **wouldn't have died**. (= The people died because the world is not a fair place.)*
*If I **spoke** Indonesian, I **would have understood** what he said. (= I didn't understand what he said, because I don't speak Indonesian.)*

Unit 8

Future continuous

1 If we want to talk about an action that will be in progress at a specified future time, we use the future continuous tense.
*Twenty years from now people **will be living** under the sea.*
*Later this month I'll **be visiting** my grandparents in Florida.*

2 The future continuous is formed by *will* + *be* + the *-ing* form of the verb.

Future perfect

1 If we want to talk about an action that will have been completed by a specified future time, we use the future perfect tense.
*By 2050 ninety per cent of the Amazon **will have vanished**.*
*By the time the World Cup finishes, I'll **have watched** more than 60 hours of soccer.*

2 The future perfect tense is formed by *will* + the present perfect.

Unit 9

Past perfect passive

1 We use the past perfect to make it very clear that a past action happened <u>before</u> another action.
*When we got to the party, James **had left**.*

2   We use the past perfect passive to say that a past action happened before another one, but also when we do not know who did the action, or that they are not important.
    *I got to the store late, and all the ice cream **had been sold**.*
    *I was surprised to find this old book. I thought it **had been thrown** away.*
    *My hometown looked different because several new stores **had been built**.*

3   The past perfect passive is formed with the past perfect of the verb *to be* (*had (not) been*) + the past participle of the main verb.

Past perfect continuous

1   We use the past perfect continuous to talk about ongoing actions that began before another action in the past.
    *When I got to the party, my friends **had been dancing** for more than an hour.*
    *Her eyes were red, so he knew that she **had been crying**.*
    *When my mother called me for dinner, I **had been reading** for two hours.*

2   The past perfect continuous is formed with the past perfect of the verb *to be* [*had (not) been*] + the *-ing* form of the main verb.

Unit 10

It as subject with infinitives

1   We often use the word *it* to introduce sentences in English, and often it does not refer to an actual thing. For example, we use *it* when we say hello:
    It's nice to meet you.

2   The structure is often *It* + *be* + adjective + infinitive with *to*.
    *It's **interesting to listen to** her ideas.*
    *It's **wonderful to see** people smile.*
    *It's **important to understand** this point.*

3   The structure can also be *It* + verb + infinitive.
    *It **hurts to see** people cry.*
    *It **feels great to be back** in the town where I was born.*

Modal verbs

1   Modal verbs say how the speaker or writer views a situation or action, in the present, the past or the future. They are used to say something about certainty, possibility, or whether something is necessary, permitted or forbidden.
    *I **might** see you tomorrow.* (possible)
    *I **will** see him tomorrow.* (certain)
    *You **must** come and see us.* (necessary)
    *You **can't** come in here.* (forbidden)

2   We use modal verbs to express a wide range of functions.
    *I think it **will** rain tonight.* (prediction)
    ***May** I come in?* ([asking for] permission)
    *They **might not** arrive on time.* (possibility)
    *You **can't** do that.* (prohibition)
    *She **can** run a marathon in three hours.* (ability)
    *I **must** remember to buy some stamps.* (obligation)
    *They **must have been** tired at the end of the race.* (deduction, past)
    *You **could** call Peter and ask him.* (suggestion)

3   All modal verbs are followed by the base form of a verb. They are auxiliaries and do not need (e.g.) *do/does/did* to make negatives and questions.

Unit 11

Phrasal verbs review

These points may help you remember how to use phrasal verbs correctly.

1   Can the phrasal verb be split?

    The verb is not split if it is intransitive (this means that the verb doesn't take an object) because there is no object.
    *We find it hard to **get by** on just one salary.* (There is no object to split *get* and *by*.)

2   If the verb is transitive, we need to know if the verb is separable or not. If it is not separable, then the two parts need to stay together.
    *The report **looks into** problems facing workers in poor countries.*
    NOT: ~~The report **looks** problems facing workers in poor countries **into**.~~

    Note how the *Cambridge Advanced Learner's Dictionary* identifies this kind of verb: *look into **sth*** (sth = something)

3   With separable phrasal verbs, the object can come between the two parts.
    *We **looked** his name **up** on the Internet.*
    *We **looked up** his name on the Internet.*

    Note how the *Cambridge Advanced Learner's Dictionary* identifies this kind of verb: *look **sth** up*

4   If we use a pronoun with a separable phrasal verb, then it must come between the two parts. *I don't believe you.*
    *You **made** it **up**.*
    NOT: ~~I don't believe you. You **made up** it.~~

5   Finally, some phrasal verbs have three (or more) parts. These cannot be split.
    *The big companies **get away with** murder.*
    *I don't know why people **put up with** it.*

Unit 12

Reduced relative clauses

When a relative clause is passive, we can leave out the relative pronoun and the verb *to be*.
*The shopping center, **(that was)** opened by the mayor, is the biggest in the country.*
*The book **(that was)** written by Madonna has become a huge success.*

Tag questions review

Tag questions are commonly used in conversation to confirm what we think is true.
*You're interested in politics, **aren't you**? (= If I remember correctly, you're interested in politics.)*

We also use tag questions to make conversation.
*Young people should show more interest in politics, **shouldn't they**? (= This is not a question but what I believe.)*

When the main clause is affirmative, the tag question is negative.
*Athletes **get** paid too much, **don't they**?*
*You **will** come to my party, **won't you**?*

Similarly, if the main clause is negative, the tag question is affirmative.
*Pop stars like Bono **can't** make a real difference, **can they**?*
*You **don't** live around here, **do you**?*

Unit 13

Indirect questions review

1   We often use indirect questions to ask people for information. They are considered more polite. Indirect questions can be statements or questions and often start with expressions like *I don't know ... I'd like to know ... I wonder ...* and *Can you find out ...*

2   When we use indirect questions, the word order that follows the question word is that of a statement and <u>not</u> a question.
    *Can you find out **when the movie starts**? (NOT: ~~Can you find out when does the movie start?~~)*
    *I don't know **what her name is**. (NOT: ~~I don't know what is her name.~~)*
    *I wonder **why she said that**. (NOT: ~~I wonder why did she say that.~~)*

3   If we are expecting a *yes/no* answer, we use *if* or *whether*.
    *Can you tell me **if** the movie has started yet?*
    *Do you know **whether** she still lives there?*

verbs + *wh-* clauses

1   When we want to be polite, we often use questions with the following phrases to ask people for information:
    Can you tell me... Can I ask you... Could you tell me... and *Do you know...*

2　These phrases are often followed by a clause starting with a question word such as *who, when, where* or *why.*
The word order that follows the question word is that of a statement and not a question.
*Can you tell me **where she'll go**?* (NOT: ~~Can you tell me where will she go?~~)
*Can I ask you **why she left**?* (NOT: ~~Can I ask you why did she leave?~~)
*Could you tell me **who that is**?* (NOT: ~~Could you tell me who is that?~~)
*Do you know **when he's leaving**?* (NOT: ~~Do you know when is he leaving?~~)

Unit 14

Participial phrases

In participial phrases, we use the *-ing* form of the verb to combine two clauses that share the same subject.
They can be used:

1　to talk about two events that happen(ed) at the same time.
Looking out *across the sea, I couldn't imagine a more beautiful view.* (= At the same time as looking out across the sea, I was also thinking about how beautiful the view was.)
Drinking *a cool lemonade, he stretched out on the sand.* (= At the same time as stretching out on the sand he was drinking a lemonade.)

2　to talk about an action that happened before the other action in the sentence.
Having paid *the bill, we left the hotel.* (= We paid the bill and then left the hotel.)
Having written *the postcard, I looked for a post office to buy a stamp.* (= I wrote the postcard and then looked for a post office.)

Note that in this case we use *having* followed by the past participle.

3　Remember, the subject of both clauses must be the same.
~~*Looking up in the sky, the moon was beautiful.*~~
This suggests the moon was looking up into the sky, which does not make sense.
Looking up in the sky, I noticed how beautiful the moon was.
This sentence is acceptable as the subject *(I)* is the same in both clauses.

4　Participial phrases are more common in writing than in spoken language.

Passive of *have to/need to*

1　We use the passive of *have to* and *need to* talk about things that are done for us. It is not always stated who is doing the action. The passive of *(not) have to* and *(not) need to* are formed by *have to/need to + be +* past participle.
*My clothes **need to be cleaned** (by someone).*
*They **have to be told** where to stand (by the teacher).*

2　Use the negative to talk about things that don't need to be done.
*The car **doesn't need to be fixed**.*
*The windows **don't have to be opened**.*

Unit 15

Passive report structures

1　We use passive report structures when we want to report information and the agent is not important.
*Chinese **is thought to be** the most spoken language in the world.* (= It is not important to say who thinks this.)

2　We commonly use passive report structures with verbs such as *say, think, believe, know* and *consider.*

3　If we use a passive report structure to talk about beliefs or knowledge in the present, we use *to be* + past participle of the reporting verb + infinitive.
*He **is believed to be** the last man who speaks this language.*
*English **is known to have** an extremely large vocabulary.*

4　If we use a passive report structure to talk about beliefs or knowledge in the past, we use *to be* + past participle of the reporting verb + *to* + present perfect.
*He **is thought to have spoken** more than 12 languages.* (= He is no longer alive.)
*They **are said to have been** a highly sophisticated animal.* (= The animal no longer exists.)

5　Passive report structures are formal and are more commonly used in news reports than in spoken language.

Unit 16

Clauses of purpose: *to / in order to / so as to*

1   When we want to give the reason why someone did something, we can use a number of different linking words, for example *to, in order to* and *so as to*.

*We arrived early **in order to** get a good seat.*

*I called him **to** cancel the appointment.*

*I told him about my problems **so as to** help him understand.*

Note that *to* is less formal than *in order to* and *so as to*.

2   When we want to make these sentences negative, we put *not* before *to*.

*He didn't tell me too much **so as not to** spoil the movie for me.*

*I didn't say anything **not to** disappoint them.*

*We left early **in order not to** get there too late.*

Result clauses with *so / such (that)*

1   We use *so / such (that)* to show how one thing is the result of another thing.

2   We use *so* with an adjective or an adverb.

*The movie was **so bad (that)** we left before the end.*

*He spoke **so quickly (that)** I didn't understand a word he said.*

3   We use *such* with a noun.

*It was **such an interesting movie (that)** I thought about it for days.*

*They are **such boring people (that)** I'd be happy never to see them again.*

Notes

Notes

Notes

Notes

Notes

Notes

Thanks and acknowledgments

The authors would like to thank a number of people whose support has proved invaluable during the planning, writing and production process of *American English in Mind*.

First of all we would like to thank the numerous teachers and students in many countries of the world who have used the first edition of *English in Mind*. Their enthusiasm for the course, and the detailed feedback and valuable suggestions we got from many of them were an important source of inspiration and guidance for us in developing the concept and in the creation of *American English in Mind*.

In particular, the authors and publishers would like to thank the following teachers who gave up their valuable time for classroom observations, interviews and focus groups:

Brazil

Warren Cragg (ASAP Idiomas); Angela Pinheiro da Cruz (Colégio São Bento; Carpe Diem); Ana Paula Vedovato Maestrello (Colégio Beatíssima Virgem Maria); Natália Mantovanelli Fontana (Lord's Idiomas); Renata Condi de Souza (Colégio Rio Branco, Higienópolis Branch); Alexandra Arruda Cardoso de Almeida (Colégio Guilherme Dumont Villares / Colégio Emilie de Villeneuve); Gisele Siqueira (Speak Up); Ana Karina Giusti Mantovani (Idéia Escolas de Línguas); Maria Virgínia G. B. de Lebron (UFTM / private lessons); Marina Piccinato (Speak Up); Patrícia Nero (Cultura Inglesa / Vila Mariana); Graziela Barroso (Associação Alumni); Francisco Carlos Peinado (Wording); Maria Lúcia Sciamarelli (Colégio Divina Providencia / Jundiaí); Deborah Hallal Jorge (Nice Time Language Center); Lilian Itzicovitch Leventhal (Colégio I. L. Peretz); Dulcinéia Ferreira (One Way Línguas); and Priscila Prieto and Carolina Cruz Marques (Seven Idiomas).

Colombia

Luz Amparo Chacón (Gimnasio Los Monjes); Mayra Barrera; Diana de la Pava (Colegio de la Presentación Las Ferias); Edgar Ardila (Col. Mayor José Celestino Mutis); Sandra Cavanzo B. (Liceo Campo David); Claudia Susana Contreras and Luz Marína Zuluaga (Colegio Anglo Americano); Celina Roldán and Angel Torres (Liceo Cervantes del Norte); Nelson Navarro; Maritza Ruiz Martín; Francisco Mejía, and Adriana Villalba (Colegio Calasanz).

Ecuador

Paul Viteri (Colegio Andino, Quito); William E. Yugsan (Golden Gate Academy– Quito); Irene Costales (Unidad Educativa Cardinal Spellman Femenino); Vinicio Sanchez and Sandra Milena Rodríguez (Colegio Santo Domingo de Guzmán); Sandra Rigazio and María Elena Moncayo (Unidad Educativa Tomás Moro, Quito); Jenny Alexandra Jara Recalde and Estanislao Javier Pauta (COTAC, Quito); Verónica Landázuri and Marisela Madrid (Unidad Educativa "San Francisco de Sales"); Oswaldo Gonzalez and Monica Tamayo (Angel Polibio Chaves School, Quito); Rosario Llerena and Tania Abad (Isaac Newton, Quito); María Fernanda Mármol Mazzini and Luis Armijos (Unidad Educativa Letort, Quito); and Diego Bastidas and Gonzalo Estrella (Colegio Gonzaga, Quito).

Mexico

Connie Alvarez (Colegio Makarenko); Julieta Zelinski (Colegio Williams); Patricia Avila (Liceo Ibero Mexicano); Patricia Cervantes de Brofft (Colegio Frances del Pedregal); Alicia Sotelo (Colegio Simon Bolivar); Patricia Lopez (Instituto Mexico, A.C.); Maria Eugenia Fernandez Castro (Instituto Oriente Arboledas); Lilian Ariadne Lozano Bustos (Universidad Tecmilenio); Maria del Consuelo Contreras Estrada (Liceo Albert Einstein); Alfonso Rene Pelayo Garcia (Colegio Tomas Alva Edison); Ana Pilar Gonzalez (Instituto Felix de Jesus Rougier); and Blanca Kreutter (Instituto Simon Bolivar).

Our heartfelt thanks go to the *American English in Mind* team for their cooperative spirit, their many excellent suggestions and their dedication, which have been characteristic of the entire editorial process: Paul Phillips, Amy E. Hawley, Jennifer Pardilla, Kelley Perrella, Eric Zuarino, Pam Harris, Kate Powers, Shireen Madon, Brigit Dermott, Kate Spencer, Heather McCarron, Keaton Babb, Roderick Gammon, Hugo Loyola, Howard Siegelman, Colleen Schumacher, Margaret Brooks, Kathryn O'Dell, Genevieve Kocienda, Eliza Jensen, Lisa Hutchins, and Lynne Robertson.

We would also like to thank the teams of educational consultants, representatives and managers working for Cambridge University Press in various countries around the world. Space does not allow us to mention them all by name here, but we are extremely grateful for their support and their commitment.

In Student's Book 2, thanks go to David Crystal for the interview in Unit 9, and to Jon Turner for giving us the idea of using the story of Ulises de la Cruz in Unit 15.

Thanks to the team at Pentacor Big for giving the book its design; the staff at CityVox for the audio recordings; and Lightning Pictures and Mannic Media for the video.

Last but not least, we would like to thank our partners, Mares and Adriana, for their support.

The authors and publishers acknowledge the following sources of copyright material and are grateful for the permissions granted. While every effort has been made, it has not always been possible to identify the sources of all the material used, or to trace all copyright holders. If any omissions are brought to our notice, we will be happy to include the appropriate acknowledgements on reprinting.

pp. 5 and 6 adapted from *The Curious Incident of the Dog in the Night-Time*;

A.P. Watt Ltd for the text on p. 29, adapted from *The Time Machine* by H.G. Wells. Reproduced by permission of A.P. Watt on behalf of the Literary Estate of H.G. Wells;

Pan Macmillan for the text on p. 30 from *The Hitchhiker's Guide to the Galaxy* by Douglas Adams. Copyright © Douglas Adams, 2005. Reproduced by permission of Pan Macmillan;

Faber & Faber and Penguin (USA) Inc for the adapted text on p. 53 from *Lord of the Flies* by William Golding. Copyright © The Estate of William Golding 1954, renewed 1982 by William Gerald Golding. Reproduced by permission of Faber and Faber Ltd and G.P. Putnam's Sons, a division of Penguin Group (USA) Inc;

Rupert Barnes for the text on p. 65 from "Artificial Languages" www.rahbarnes.co.uk. Reproduced with permission;

Penguin Books and United Agents for the text on p. 77 from *High Fidelity* by Nick Hornby (Penguin Books 2000). Copyright © Nick Hornby 1996. By permission of United Agents Ltd (www.unitedagents.co.uk) on behalf of the author and Penguin Books Ltd;

Musiced for the adapted text on p. 83 from "The Origins of Music" www.musiced.org.uk. Reproduced by permission of Musiced.org.uk;

Text on p. 89 "Sanitation" adapted from BBC News Online. http://www.bbc.co.uk/news.

The publishers are grateful to the following illustrators: Anna Lazareva c/o Lemonade, David Shephard c/o Bright, Pat Murray (Graham Cameron Illustration), RedJelly, Rosa Dodd c/o NB Illustration, Tracey Knight c/o Lemonade, Paul McCaffrey (Sylvie Poggio), pp. 5 and 6 used by permission of Random House, Inc.

Thanks and acknowledgments

The publishers are grateful to the following for permission to reproduce photographic material:

Key: l = left, c = centre, r = right, t = top, b = bottom.

Marcinski p 65, /©Worldspec /NASA p 46; Corbis p 54, /©Nigel Pavitt/JAI p 52 (l), /Reuters/Issei Kato p 52 (r); Getty Images/AFP p 83 (t), /AFP/Jacques Demarthon p 18(tr), /AFP/ Gyln Kirk p 18 (br), /AFP/William West p 18 (cl), /Hulton Archive/Imagno p 32 (l), /Hulton Archive /London Stereoscopic Company p 32 (br), / Michael Ochs Archives p 35 (br), /Redferns/C Brandon p 72 (l), / Time & Life Pictures/Ralph Morse p 32 (tr), /Mark Venema p 59 (b), /WireImage /Paul Natkin p 35 (tc); Guardian News & Media Ltd 2005/David Levene p 36; iStockphoto/hannerjo p 83 (bl), / pixdeluxe p 52, /YinYang p 42; Kobal Collection/ITV Global/ Brian Hamill p 96 (tl), /PARAMOUNT/Melinda Sue Gordon p 96 (r), /TOUCHSTONE/SPYGLASS ENTERTAINMENT p 30, / UNIVERSAL/Ron Batzdorff p 96 (bl); Front cover in its entirety of The TIME MACHINE by H. G. Wells (Penguin Books, 2005). Text copyright © the Literary Executors of the Estate of H. G. Wells. Reproduced with permission of Penguin Books Ltd p 29; Photolibrary.com/Afl o Foto Agency/Nick Walker p 18 (cr), / Age fotostock/Henry Beeker p 84 (l), /Age fotostock/Jennifer B Waters p 84 (br), / Peter Arnold Images/Jacques Jangoux p 83 (br), / Corbis p 57, /Imagebroker.net/jspix jspix p 83 (cl), / Nordic Photos/Frank Chmura p 80, /Still Pictures/ Jorgen Schytte p 89, /WaterFrame – Underwater Images/Masa Ushioda p 84 (tr); Press Association Images/AP/Winslow Townson p 78; Rex Features pp 35 (br), 75 (r), /Ian Dickson p 35 (tl), /Everett Collection p 72 (cr), /Neale Haynes p 18 (tl), /Dezo Hoffmann p 35 (bc), /Nile Jorgensen p 14, /George Konig p 35 (bl), /Most Wanted p 72 (cl), /NBCUPHOTOBANK p 59 (t), /PIERLUIGI p 72 (r), /Brian Rasic p 75 (l), /Sipa Press p 68, /Startraks Photo p 69; Show Racism The Red Card www.theredcard.org p 39; Shutterstock Images/Andresr p 74, / Christian Musat p 86, / Vlad61 p 83 (cr).

AETN p 11, The Washington Post via Getty Images /John McDonnell p 17, Newcom/ Agencia EL UNIVERSAL/ ESPECIAL p 33 (t), KOBAL COLLECTION/ PARAMOUNT p 33 (l), Getty Images/Amana Productions p 33 (r), Alamy/I love images p 41 (tl), Getty Images/Brand X Pictures/Jupiter Images p 41 (tc), The Star Ledger/ Photo by Eunice Lee p 41 (tr), Alamy/Ron Buskirk p 41 (bl), Newscom/Diversity p 41 (br), AP Photo/Peter Kramer p 66.